COUNTDOWN TO GCSE

CHEMISTRY

Senior Assistant   ools),

M

MACMILLAN
EDUCATION

First published 1987

Published by
MACMILLAN EDUCATION LTD
Houndmills, Basingstoke, Hampshire RG21 2XS
and London
Companies and representatives
throughout the world

Printed in Great Britain by
Cox & Wyman Ltd
Reading

Designed by
Plum Design
Southampton

British Library Cataloguing in Publication Data
Slater, Bryan
Chemistry. – (Countdown to GCSE)
1. Chemistry – Study and teaching (Secondary) – Great Britain.
2. General Certificate of Secondary Education
I. Title   II. Series
540'.76   QD49.G7
ISBN 0-333-41857-3

CONTENTS
Countdown to GCSE: Chemistry

ACKNOWLEDGEMENTS

The author and publishers wish to acknowledge the following sources:

HMSO for extracts from The National Criteria by permission of the Controller of Her Majesty's Stationery Office; also
London and East Anglian Group; Midland Examining Group; Northern Examining Association; Southern Examining Group; Welsh Joint Education Committee.

The publishers have made every effort to trace the copyright holders, but if they have inadvertently overlooked any, they will be pleased to make the necessary arrangements at the first opportunity.

SECTION I
What is GCSE, and why has it come about?

The most important thing for a student to know about the GSCE examination is how to go about getting the best possible grade. Most of this book is aimed at helping those studying for GCSE chemistry to do just that.

But GCSE as a whole is a completely new system of examining, and GCSE chemistry is part of that whole. To understand what GCSE examinations are, it helps to know a little about how the system has come about, and what went before it.

'GCSE'

GCSE stands for 'General Certificate of Secondary Education'. From the initials it looks as though GCSE is a simple joining together of the General Certificate of Education (GCE) and the Certificate of Secondary Education (CSE). There are a number of reasons why this is not the case. In the first place, GCE was designed for the most able 20% of the 16-year-olds, with CSE covering the next 40% of the population. GCSE is for all these students, and more.

	Most able 20%	Next 40%	Remaining 40%
	↓	↓	↓
Before 1988	GCE	CSE	no examination
After 1988	—————————— GCSE ——————————		

One advantage, then of GCSE is that it allows more youngsters to leave with some formal qualification, which is so necessary in the modern world. This does not mean that 'standards have been lowered' to allow in less able students, however. But even more importantly, GCSE is very different from both GCE and CSE in the way it rewards what students can do. Teachers, students, parents and employers will have to adapt to this change, which will be explained shortly. But first of all, why was it necessary for there to be a change in the first place?

1

WHAT CAME BEFORE GCSE?

As we have just seen, before GCSE there was GCE and CSE. Before that, there was the School Certificate. In order to be awarded a School Certificate, a student had to do well in a number of subject areas at the same time. Less than five subjects at a 'pass' level, and the student obtained no School Certificate. GCE allowed a certificate for each individual subject to be obtained, no matter how many.

SCHOOL CERTIFICATE		GCE French	etc.
		GCE Maths	etc.
		GCE History	etc.

So GCE helped a student get more reward for what he/she could do. But it was still very difficult to reach the minimum level for getting a certificate, even if this could now be subject-by-subject.

The Certificate of Secondary Education (CSE) went a long way towards changing this, and many more students were able to leave school with something to show for their work. However, this left the schools with two systems running side-by-side. On the one hand, there was the GCE which was organised and run by universities, or groups of universities. It has always been a criticism of GCE that the universities set the standard for GCE in relation to what students would need to know to go on to do Advanced Level GCE, which in turn would let them go on to a university. So the universities have had a very heavy influence on what is taught in schools, based on their own entry standards.

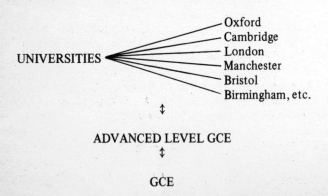

UNIVERSITIES — Oxford
— Cambridge
— London
— Manchester
— Bristol
— Birmingham, etc.

↕

ADVANCED LEVEL GCE
↕

GCE

CSE was not run by universities, but rather by groups of teachers and their employers, the Local Education Authorities, in conjunction with CSE 'Boards'. However, CSE was still heavily influenced by GCE, because it tended to copy it, and so many people came to criticise CSE as being a 'watered down GCE'.

WHY CHANGE THINGS?

Apart from the criticism that GCE, and through GCE, CSE, were too heavily influenced by the needs of only a tiny fraction of those at school, there have been a number of changes since CSE came into being. Each of these, in its own way, has increased the need for a change in the system of examination for 16-year-olds.

Perhaps the most important has been the move away from selection at the age of 11, and the introduction of Comprehensive Secondary Schools. The great majority of secondary age children in this country now go to comprehensive schools. This means that one school now has to cater for the needs of students of all abilities under one roof. As time goes by, the artificial and wasteful dividing-up of students into those studying for GCE and those studying for CSE has seemed increasingly irrelevant to the needs of the students themselves. People, obviously, do not fall neatly into separate groups. So, while many comprehensive schools have achieved a very high success rate for all their students, they have done so by overcoming the in-built awkwardness of a dual system of examinations – a constant and heavy burden.

The second important change has been the raising of the school leaving age. It is perhaps too easily forgotten that when GCE was the only examination available, children could leave school at 14. And most did – with no qualifications. The school leaving age was raised, first to 15 and then to 16. So now all stay at school until the age at which examinations can be taken. The need, therefore, is for a system which makes sense and has some relevance for everyone at the end of their compulsory schooling. But what are the needs of 16-year-olds today? Although they are able to leave the education system at 16, fewer and fewer do. And of these few, only a minority leave school and go straight into a job. So, while the examinations at 16 must, on the one hand, allow for a meaningful end to the compulsory schooling for all students, they must equally act as a foundation and preparation for other types of learning to come.

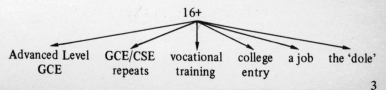

16+

Advanced Level GCE   GCE/CSE repeats   vocational training   college entry   a job   the 'dole'

WHAT WE MEAN BY 'ACCREDITATION'

It is because the needs of 16-year-olds have changed so much that the examinations you take at school have had to change so much. In the future, GCSE will not be the only evidence of a student's work by the age of 16. It will be part of an overall picture, built up of a number of different types of evidence.

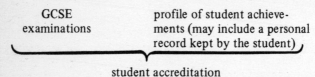

GCSE examinations | profile of student achievements (may include a personal record kept by the student)

student accreditation

Work is now going on to develop what are called 'profiles', which will be used by schools as a way of charting the progress of individuals as they develop their abilities in different areas of the curriculum. All school leavers will eventually take with them a profile of their achievements, as well as the results of their GCSE examinations.

Part of what a student's profile in mathematical skills might look like

The main part of your student profile will probably be taken up by assessments, made by your teachers, of your work, subject-by-subject, and also of your general skills. These assessments will show how you have made progress, in carefully defined ways, over a period of time. So it will be possible to see how you have learned, and the stages you have reached, when you come to leave the school. In this way, all students will receive credit for what they can do. And what they can do will be clearly shown.

Part of what a student's profile in mathematical skills might look like

Can solve simple quadratic equations		
Can solve simultaneous equations with three variables		
Can solve simultaneous equations with two variables	✓	J. Wood 10.11.88
Can solve simple algebraic equations	✓	I. Jones 27.06.88

Can use tangent, sine and cosine to find unknowns in right-angle triangles	✓	B. Brown 14-03-88
Can multiply and divide decimals using calculator	✓	A. Smith. 21.12.88
Can multiply and divide whole numbers accurately	✓	D PATEL 02.10.88
Can add and subtract accurately	✓	D SYLVIAN 31.05 87

So the word 'accreditation' has become more common than the word 'examination' when talking about the way students are assessed, because all students receive credit. The GCSE examinations are based on similar ideas to these. For this reason, they are very different from the GCE and CSE examinations.

	Grade A	Grade B	Grade C	Grade D
GCE and CSE	Came in the top Z% of those who took the exam	Came in the next Y% of those who took the exam	Came in the next X% of those who took the exam	Came in the next W% of those who took the exam
GCSE	Can do the following things ·········· ·········· ·········· ·········· ··········	Can do the following things ·········· ·········· ·········· ·········· ··········	Can do the following things ·········· ·········· ·········· ·········· ··········	Can do the following things ·········· ·········· ·········· ·········· ··········

In GCE or CSE examinations, the grade a student gained was based on the number of marks he/she obtained in the examination overall. The marks of all the students were then compared, and it was decided where to set the boundary between the grades so that a certain percentage of students got the top grade, a certain percentage got the next grade, and so on. So, two different students taking the same exam could obtain identical grades when one was good at one type of thing and the other was good at something else. This meant that there was no way of

5

telling from the grade obtained in a given subject just exactly what a student could not do. For instance, what information did a student, the student's parents and a potential employer get from the award of a Grade 'C' in GCE chemistry? Only that, right across the subject, the individual in question did not obtain as many marks as students who got a Grade 'B', but more than those who got Grade 'D'. Not much detail at the end of 11 years of school, was it!

In contrast to this, examinations under the title of GCSE are designed to give each individual student the chance to show what he or she *knows, understands and can do* in each subject. It no longer makes sense to talk about 'passing' or 'failing', since there is no dividing line between the two. Also, students are no longer compared with each other after the examination, but with criteria of performance which have been laid down beforehand, and which are known to all concerned.

So, a GCSE grade in chemistry can be translated into a list of 'can do's'. Taken together with the profile which a student will leave school with, GCSE grades give a much clearer picture of what an individual can do, and each student gets credit for what they have achieved. In this way, the new patterns of accreditation for 16-year-olds will serve all youngsters better, because the needs of any single group will not dictate the way assessments are made about the rest. All will be judged in the same way, within a clear and logical framework, which will be understandable to parents, employers and other educational establishments alike. Perhaps most important of all, it will be understandable to the students themselves.

KEY POINTS FROM SECTION 1

1. GCSE is designed with many more students than were covered by the old GCE and CSE in mind.

2. In GCSE, individuals will receive credit for what they can do, without reference to the performance of others.

3. GCSE will form part of a more detailed pattern of accreditation at 16+, which will include student profiles.

SECTION 2
The aims of GCSE chemistry

How does GCSE work, and how does GCSE chemistry fit into the overall examination pattern? For the purposes of GCSE, the groups of universities which look after GCE and the different CSE Boards have all been grouped together into just five 'Examining Groups'. Each examining group is made up of an old GCE component and an old CSE component.

Each of the five examining groups is able to devise its own syllabus and set its own examinations in each subject. So there are GCSE chemistry syllabuses which come from five different sources - four in England and one in Wales (Scotland has its own system of examinations):

NEA   Northern Examining Association
MEG   Midland Examining Group
SEG   Southern Examining Group
LEAG   London and East Anglian Examining Group
WJEC   Welsh Joint Education Committee

Your own school will have decided to use the chemistry syllabus and examinations of one of these five examining groups.

NATIONAL CRITERIA

But the examining groups cannot simply put anything they want into their chemistry syllabuses. Instead, every GCSE chemistry syllabus has to fit into a set of rules which have been laid down in advance. These rules are called National Criteria.

This is another important change which has come with GCSE. It is really the first time that we have decided, across the country as a whole, exactly what the content of each of the different subjects studied at school shall be. Before GCSE, there could be big differences between the chemistry syllabus and examinations set by one board - say London University - and those set by another, such as Oxford University.

In the first place, there are criteria which cover all the different GCSE syllabuses, in all the different subjects. These are called the GCSE

General Criteria. Then there are National Criteria for all the science subjects, and finally, National Criteria for chemistry itself.

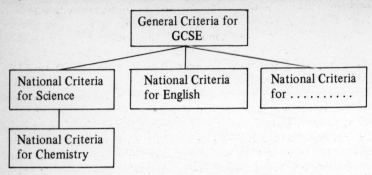

So your GCSE chemistry syllabus will have been designed to fit in with the rules for chemistry, for all the science subjects, and for all the subjects in GCSE. What does all this mean as far as what you learn at school and your GCSE examinations are concerned?

GCSE CHEMISTRY AND GCSE SCIENCE

We cannot look at GCSE chemistry on its own. It must be considered as part of what GCSE means for the whole science curriculum. As we shall see, science teaching is on the brink of some major changes, and GCSE science has been designed to help these come about. But what is it about the science that is taught in schools at the moment that means that there have to be changes? And what are the nature of these changes facing science, and therefore chemistry?

For most children in the first two years of secondary school, science is taught either as all three separate sciences side by side, or as an integrated single subject. In the third year it is normal for most students to learn physics, chemistry and biology as separate subjects, and at the end of the year to make a decision on their 'options' for years four and five. Normally, this means choosing one, two or three of the separate sciences.

Many schools insist that all students learn at least one science subject. Unfortunately, this has all too frequently meant that two science subjects have been 'dropped', and girls in particular have tended to continue with only one subject (usually biology) in years four and five.

This imbalance in the science that is learned in school was picked out as a particular difficulty by the Government's statement of policy on the science curriculum offered in schools, in 1985. This took as its starting point the need for education to prepare the next generation to enter and inherit a rapidly changing world of science and technology.

8

Schools have to begin the scientific education of tomorrow's scientists and technologists, but it is as important that they also give a general background of scientific understanding to all future citizens. It is important to recognise, therefore, that science is about more than knowledge alone; it is also about a way of thinking. Because that way of thinking helps us to look critically at what we believe, to weigh evidence and to make informed choices, it increases individual autonomy and awareness. It makes a 'wholer' person, and that is the principal aim of education.

For that reason, it is important that everybody receives a broad base of scientific education at school, whether or not they are going to become scientists themselves. It is also important that science education should not begin only when children reach the age of 11, as has tended to happen up until the present time. It should begin in the earliest years of school and continue at least until the age of 16. The Government's policy statement for the science curriculum was given the title 'Science 5 to 16' to emphasise that very point.

As well as pointing to the many good things happening in schools, 'Science 5 to 16' posed a number of serious questions which sprang from its survey of current practice in schools, and which need to be answered if Britain is to have enough trained scientists and a scientifically aware population in the next century:

1 Why do too few girls (only about one in five) study physics after the age of 13?
2 Why do too few boys (only about one in three) study biology after the age of 13?
3 Why do too few students (only about one in four) study elements of each of the three main sciences after the age of 13?

Science is certainly thought of as being a 'difficult' subject by both students and their teachers. There is no doubt that this is linked to the nature of the science courses being offered in schools, which combine a need to learn many facts with the need to master a number of abstract ideas. This has come about because the content of science courses has been changing for the last twenty-or-so years. 'Traditional' science courses have been added to by curriculum projects, designed for different stages of secondary school and for different ability levels, which have placed more emphasis on students developing their own understanding during lessons. So instead of science being a set of facts to be learned, in which you carry out experiments only to 'prove' something which you have been told is true (as tended to happen in 'traditional' science teaching), there has been a steady change towards a view of science which lets you find your own answers to questions which you yourself have posed. In other words, the emphasis has moved away

Science curriculum projects

	Science 5–13	Nuffield 'O' level	Nuffield Combined Science	SCISP*	Nuffield Secondary Science	LAMP†
Age	5–13	11–16	11–13	13–16	13–16	13–16
Ability range designed for	all	top 20–25%	all	top 20–25%	middle	all
Date of introduction	1972	1966–7	1970	1973–4	1971	1976

*Schools Council Integrated Science Project
†Science for the Less Academically Motivated Pupil

from the simple learning of facts to the development of scientific understanding. It is now probably fair to say that all but the most traditional of science teachers and science syllabuses have been influenced by these ideas to a greater or lesser extent. However, science courses still contain large amounts of factual information which you have to assimilate alongside your developing understanding of the ideas of science.

How, then, are students coping with the demands now being made of them in school science? Until recently, there has been very little to go on in the form of hard evidence in this area. However, recent reports by the Government-funded Assessment of Performance Unit, and follow-up work carried out by the Children's Learning in Science Project (at the University of Leeds), have thrown up some important insights. For instance, it was shown that, for a representative sample of 15-year-olds studying science:

1 Ability to apply the concepts of physics, chemistry and biology to new contexts was very low.
2 The ability to estimate was low. This meant that pupils find it difficult to select measuring instruments appropriate to the magnitude of the quantity to be measured. They also have difficulty in developing a 'feel' for whether answers are sensible or not.
3 39% failed to read a ruler to within 1 mm accuracy, and 42% failed to read a stopclock to within 1 second accuracy. Errors of this sort must lead to difficulties in interpreting experimental data.
4 Pupils demonstrated markedly improved performance in tests of practical skills when allowed to carry out actual practical work, than they did in pencil and paper tests of practical tasks.

Particularly of concern was the finding that students are poor at applying the scientific ideas which they have learned. The success or otherwise of the development of scientific understanding depends on a number of interacting factors, and it is not fully understood. But we know that some ideas are inherently more difficult to grasp than others, and that the intellectual abilities of children are changing very rapidly during the period of secondary schooling – when most science is learned. Ideally, it might be possible to match the difficulty of scientific ideas to which students are being introduced and their developing capabilities. However, this is no easy matter, since it is most certainly true that different individuals show evidence of the same emerging mental abilities in different areas and at different rates. We also have no simple way of knowing precisely how difficult a given idea expressed or presented in a certain way actually is. Indeed, the evidence is that it is in fact the way that an idea is presented which has as much to do with its difficulty for the learner as anything else. Of particular importance, it seems, is the relevance and interest which the idea holds for the learner, and this has too often been neglected in the design of science courses so far.

So, the picture which has emerged is one in which children at school are not deriving all that they might from science courses at school, for the following reasons:

1 Science courses may contain ideas which are too difficult and these may not be presented in a form which seems relevant to the needs of the children learning them. There may also be too great a burden of factual content in science syllabuses to allow pupils time to encounter scientific ideas in ways which will make them easier to master.
2 Too few pupils, especially girls, follow a balanced science curriculum to the age of 16.
3 Teachers may over-estimate the basic skills which their pupils possess.
4 Traditional pencil and paper methods of assessing what pupils know may not do them justice.

'Science 5 to 16' pointed to the changes which are needed. This document, which we can think of as a 'science pupils' charter', contains the following points:

1 Each pupil is entitled to a programme of science education which incorporates substantial elements from each of the three main sciences, up to the age of 16.
2 A maximum of 20% of school time should be spent on science beyond the age of 13 (less time than is now spent by the minority of pupils who study all three sciences in years four and five), to ensure that all pupils receive a balanced curriculum.

11

3 Unnecessary factual content will have to be eliminated, in order that courses give pupils the opportunity fully to develop their scientific competence by means of
   (a) making observations;
   (b) selecting which observations to make so that these are relevant to their investigations;
   (c) seeking and identifying patterns and relating these to patterns perceived earlier;
   (d) suggesting and evaluating explanations of these patterns;
   (e) designing and carrying out experiments;
   (f) communicating verbally, mathematically and graphically;
   (g) handling equipment safely and effectively;
   (h) using knowledge in conducting investigations;
   (i) bringing their knowledge to bear in attempting to solve theoretical problems.
4 Science education should draw exclusively on the everyday experience of children, and should involve the technological applications and social consequences of science at all stages.
5 The science for lower attaining pupils should not be different in kind from that provided for the more able. It should, however, enable all students to achieve worthwhile success.
6 Schools will need to organise their curriculum in years four and five in such a way that these aims can be met.

How have these goals been translated into reality by the design of GSCE chemistry?

AIMS OF GCSE CHEMISTRY

When we talk about the educational 'aims' of a course or a lesson at school, we mean the educational purpose which it fulfils. The National Criteria for GCSE give the general requirements which all GCSE subjects must fulfil. One of these is that for a given subject like chemistry, its own aims must fit in with the overall aims for GCSE science.

So, both GCSE science and GCSE chemistry have a set of aims. The aims in the National Criteria for science are spelled out in more detail in the aims within the National Criteria for chemistry. For instance:

Science aim

To provide through well designed studies of experimental and practical science a worthwhile educational experience for all pupils whether or not they go on to study science beyond this level. . . .

Chemistry aim

To provide a body of chemical knowledge appropriate for students
1 **Not studying the subject beyond this stage**
2 **Continuing further studies in Chemistry.**

So chemistry, like all the other sciences, must be a meaningful and useful course of study for those who will not go on studying it beyond GCSE level. And it must also prepare those who will go on to study at a higher level in future years. This means that your chemistry course for GCSE has to be designed to give you an understanding of the basic ideas of the subject, but it must also make sense in itself. It cannot simply be a collection of unrelated facts and theories. You should be able to feel that you have some kind of a 'whole' picture of what chemistry is about at the end of your course. What's more, you should find your chemistry 'interesting' and 'enjoyable'.

Science aim	*Chemistry aim*
... and, in particular, to enable them to acquire sufficient understanding and knowledge	
1 to become confident citizens in a technological world, able to take or develop an informed interest in matters of scientific import;	
2 to recognise the usefulness, and limitations, of scientific method and appreciate its applicability in other disciplines and in everyday life;	
3 to be suitably prepared for studies beyond the GCSE level in pure sciences, in applied sciences or in science-dependent vocational courses.	**To provide a body of chemical knowledge appropriate for students** *3* studying related subjects, at the same or different levels.

GCSE chemistry has to help you to see how science is part of everyday life. You should remember things you have learned in chemistry long after you have finished studying the subject, because you should constantly see how its ideas explain the world around you. Examples might be why steel (and not sodium) is used in building cars and bridges, how washing-up liquid works and how we are able to make it, why plastics are so useful and where we get them from, how it can be that energy is stored in chemicals (such as petrol), the chemical basis of photography ... and many, many more.

Chemistry is about some of the basic things which affect our lives. So what you learn in GCSE chemistry should help you throughout your life. It should help you to make up your own mind about issues such as whether lead should be banned from petrol, whether we should use nuclear fuels as we do, whether the cost we pay in terms of pollution and the using up of our natural resources is worth it for the increase in comfort which we get, and many others.

You should also understand what makes a science a science, and how it might be possible to use the ideas behind the 'scientific method' in other areas of school work and in life in general. You should know what it means to 'be scientific' about something – and when you can be scientific, and when you can't!

In addition, your chemistry must equip you to learn other subjects, such as biology, at GCSE level or higher, as well as giving you the chemistry which you need for subjects like geology or engineering, or courses of training to become an animal nurse, a photographer, a pharmacist, a hairdresser or a motor mechanic.

So whether you are going on for further studies in the future, or whether you are going to end your school career after GCSE, your GCSE chemistry should have left you with a clearer picture of part of the world.

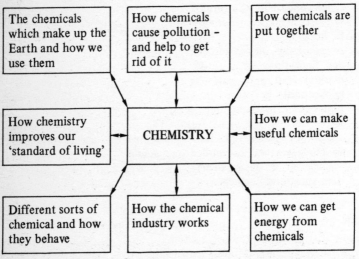

As well as this type of understanding, your GCSE chemistry should also have given you skills and abilities which are related to learning science, but which are also valuable tools for everyday living:

Science aim	*Chemistry aim*
To develop abilities and skills that *1* are relevant to the study and practice of science;	To promote in students an acquisition of knowledge and understanding of chemical patterns and principles.

2 are useful in everyday life;
3 encourage safe practice

To encourage students to apply their chemical knowledge and understanding to familiar and unfamiliar situations.

To develop students' abilities to interpret, organise, and evaluate data in order to make decisions and solve problems.

To develop students' ability to communicate in appropriate ways.

To develop students' abilities to perform experiments, having due regard for safety.

So, as well as helping you to understand the nature of science, and through that to understand better the world in which we live, GCSE chemistry should also be developing your scientific (chemical) competence, in ways which leave you with skills which are useful outside the study of science. Knowing how to work safely, applying what you know to new situations, making decisions, solving problems and being able to communicate with others are all vital parts of 'being a scientist'. They are also extremely useful abilities to have when you are not 'being a scientist'. How GCSE chemistry will help you to develop these skills will depend on the way in which you learn the subject at school. This, in turn, will depend upon the way the new examinations will assess what you know, as we shall see shortly.

But, as well as giving you the skills which you can pick up through studying a science subject, GCSE chemistry should also give you an interest and enjoyment in the very nature of science itself:

Science aim

To simulate curiosity, interest and enjoyment in science and its methods of enquiry.

Chemistry aim

To make students aware of the importance to scientific method of accurate experimental work.

To develop students' skills of observation and their ability to record and interpret their observations.

To develop students' abilities to form hypotheses and design experiments to test these hypotheses.

15

So your GCSE chemistry course has to be designed so that you will learn, through what you do, how science goes about gaining new information and trying to find patterns and explanations for known facts.

Yet you should also see how our understanding in science, and how we use what we know, are both affected by outside influences:

Science aim

To promote an awareness that the study and practice of science are co-operative and cumulative activities and are subject to social economic, technological, ethical and cultural influences and limitations

and

**To stimulate interest in, and care for, the environment.
To promote an awareness that the applications of sciences may be both beneficial and detrimental to the individual, the community and the environment.**

Chemistry aim

To encourage students to appreciate the developing and sometimes transitory nature of chemical knowledge, principles and models

and

To develop students' appreciation of the scientific, social, economic, environmental and technological contributions and applications of chemistry.

In other words chemistry, and other sciences, cannot exist 'in a vacuum'. They are, and should be, influenced by the stage of development we have reached so far, by the world as it is today, and by the value which people place on science and its products.

KEY POINTS FROM SECTION 2

1. Five examining Groups for GCSE have been set up for England and Wales, and each has a GCSE chemistry syllabus.

2 All chemistry syllabuses must fit in with the aims laid down for chemistry itself, and for science as a whole, nationally.

3 GCSE science subjects (and therefore GCSE chemistry) have been designed in such a way that they help overcome the problems that have been shown to exist with school science at present.

They will also help to introduce the kind of scheme in schools laid down by the Government's statement of policy 'Science, 5 to 16'.

SECTION 3
The content of GCSE chemistry

The aims of GCSE chemistry in the National Criteria describe, in a general way, what studying the subject should do for you – in terms of what you know, understand and can do at the end of the course. But when it comes to *testing* what you have learned, some more specific goals need to be laid down. The National Criteria contain a set of assessment objectives, which have been worked out from the aims of GCSE chemistry. These assessment objectives are designed to do the following things:

1 Lay down in a clear form what the syllabus should contain.
2 Describe what you can be tested on in the GCSE examination.
3 Give a guide to *how* you should be tested.

Every student, whatever their ability, will be tested right across the assessment objectives. How well you meet these objectives in the examination will decide what grade you get. The full list is given below.

ASSESSMENT OBJECTIVES IN GCSE CHEMISTRY

1 Experimental work

Candidates should be able to:
1.1 follow instructions for practical work;

1.2 select appropriate apparatus;

1.3 handle and manipulate chemical apparatus and material safely;

1.4 make accurate observations and measurements, being aware of possible sources of error;

1.5 record accurately and clearly the results of experiments;

1.6 draw conclusions and make generalisations from experiments;

1.7 plan and organise simple experimental investigations to test hypotheses.

2 Recall/knowledge

Candidates should be able to recall:

2.1 chemical terminology, symbolism, units and conventions;

2.2 chemical facts;

2.3 experimental techniques, procedures and safe laboratory working practices;

2.4 chemical principles, concepts, theories, laws, models, patterns and generalisations;

2.5 everyday applications and uses of the knowledge covered by 2.1 to 2.4

2.6 social, economic, environmental and technological implications of the knowledge covered by 2.1 to 2.5.

3 Understanding

Candidates should be able to:

3.1 explain their knowledge in terms of the relevant principles, concepts, theories, definitions, laws, models, patterns and generalisations;

3.2 present, use and interpret chemical data/information in diagrammatic, symbolic, graphical, numerical or written form and translate information from one form to another;

3.3 explain practical techniques, procedures and safe laboratory working practices;

3.4 perform numerical calculations in which guidance on the method of solution is provided;

3.5 explain everyday applications and uses of chemistry;

3.6 explain the social economic, environmental and technological implications of chemistry.

4 Application, analysis, synthesis and evaluation

Candidates should, with reference to familiar and unfamiliar situations, be able to:

4.1 apply appropriate chemical principles, concepts, theories, definitions, laws, models and patterns to interpret, draw conclusions and make generalisations and predictions from chemical facts, observations and experimental data;

4.2 select appropriate facts to illustrate a given chemical principle, concept, theory, model or pattern;

4.3 present chemical ideas in a clear and logical form;

18

4.4 select and organise data and perform calculations in which guidance on the method of solution is not provided;

4.5 select tests, procedures and practical techniques to investigate the validity of interpretations, conclusions, generalisations and predictions;

4.6 evaluate the social, economic, environmental and technological implications of chemistry.

The content of GCSE chemistry, the actual chemical facts and ideas which it contains, are intended to be a vehicle for letting students show how they have met the assessment objectives. So there is a relationship between the aims of GCSE chemistry, the assessment objectives, and the content:

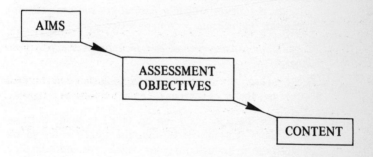

SYLLABUS CONTENT

The National Criteria for GCSE chemistry lay down a minimum core of content which must be in any syllabus. This is as follows:

1 Experimental work
Manipulating; observing; measuring; recording; designing; interpreting.

2 Elements and compounds
Study of the following elements and their compounds. Hydrogen, helium, carbon, nitrogen, oxygen, neon, sodium, magnesium, aluminium, sulphur, chlorine, argon, potasssium, calcium, iron, copper, zinc, bromine and iodine.

19

3 Ideas, models, patterns and theories

Patterns and classifications:

> solid, liquid, gas
> pure substance and mixtures
> elements and compounds
> metals and non-metals
> the reactivity series
> the periodic table
> acids, bases, salts, pH

Atomic structure and bonding; energetics; reversible reactions; speed of reaction; oxidation and reduction; electrochemistry; quantitative chemistry.

4 Chemistry in industry

Extraction of metals; oxygen, nitrogen, carbon dioxide; ammonia; mineral acids; petroleum products; natural gas and coal; ethanol, sodium chloride and calcium carbonate; water.

5 Social, economic, environmental and technological applications of chemistry

Making the most of the world's resources; pollution control; food supply; uses and abuses of substances; energy resources.

Up to half as much material again can be added to make the final syllabus – but no more. The idea is to limit the total amount in the syllabus so that there is enough time for developing understanding, gaining skills and learning about the way chemistry works. This can be in the form of a greater depth of treatment of core material, or as new material, or as a mixture of both.

Experimental work is seen as being very important in GCSE chemistry, so it is placed first in the list of core content. It must be used to illustrate the whole of the GCSE chemistry syllabus, including technological aspects.

So each GCSE chemistry syllabus has to fall within this pattern:

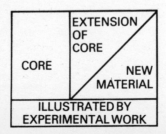

COMPARISON OF GCSE CHEMISTRY SYLLABUSES

Final GCSE Chemistry syllabuses are available, as follows:

Northern Examining Association (NEA) - one syllabus (together with a second proposed syllabus, to be designated syllabus B, on the revised Nuffield chemistry materials)

Midland Examining Group (MEG) - two syllabuses

- chemistry
- chemistry (Nuffield)

London and East Anglia Examining Group (LEAG) - two syllabuses

- syllabus A
- syllabus B (based on revised Nuffield Chemistry materials)

Southern Examining Group (SEG) - two syllabuses

- chemistry
- chemistry (alternative) (based on revised Nuffield Chemistry materials)

Welsh Joint Education Committee (WJEC) - one syllabus

You can get copies of the actual syllabuses from the following addresses:

NEA : Joint Matriculation Board, Manchester, M15 6EU.
MEG : Oxford and Cambridge School Examinations Board, Trumpington Street, Cambridge, CD2 1QB.
LEAG : University of London School Examinations Council, Stewart House, 32 Russell Square, London, WC1B 5DN.
SEG : Southern Regional Examinations Board, Avondale House, 33 Carlton Crescent, Southampton, SO9 4YL.
WJEC : 245 Western Avenue, Cardiff, Wales, CF5 2YX.

In the following analysis of the contents of these syllabuses, these symbols have been used:

*　　　　will only appear in extension papers
OPT　　only appears in optional work
◄(OPT)　included in main syllabus but treated in much greater depth in optional work

You should find out from your teacher which syllabus it is that you are following.

Chemical substances

	NEA	MEG	Nuffield	LEAG A	LEAG B	SEG	SEG Alt.	WJEC
Pure substances/mixtures	•	•	•	•	•	•	•	•
States of matter (solid/ liquid/gas)	•	•	•	•	•	•	•	•
Colloids			OPT	OPT				
Structure of solids								
metals	•	•	*	•	OPT	•	•	•
ionic compounds	•	•	•	•	•	•	•	•
molecular compounds	•	•	•	•	•	•	•	•
giant structures	•	•	•	•	•	•	•	•
Behaviour of liquids	•	•	•	•		•	•	•
Behaviour of solutions	•					•		
Behaviour of gases	•	•	•	•				•
Elements and compounds	•	•	•	•	•	•		•
Metals and non-metals								
their properties	•	•	•	•	•	•	•	•
Metals studied in detail:								
group 1	•	•	•	•	•	•	•	•
group 2	•		•	•	•	•	•	•
transition metals			•	•		*	•	
iron	•	•	•	•	•(OPT)	•	•	•
copper	•	•	•	•	•	•	•	•
zinc	•	•	•	•	•(OPT)	•	•	•
sodium	•	•	•	•	•	•	•	•
magnesium	•	•	•	•		•	•	•
aluminium	•	•	•	•		•	•	•
lead		•			OPT	•	•	•
Extraction of metals from compounds related to reactivity	*	•	•	•	•	•	•	•
Non-metals studied in detail:								
carbon	•	•	•			•	•	•
simple carbon compounds (organic)	•	•	•	•	•	•	•	•
homologous series	•	•	•	•	•	•	•	•
isomerism	*	•						
carbon in biosphere	•				•	•	•	•
simple carbon compounds (inorganic)	•	•	•	•	•	•	•	•
nitrogen	•	•	•	•	•	•	•	•
nitrogen in biosphere	•	•	•	•	•	•	•	•
simple nitrogen compounds	•	•	•	•	•	•	•	•

	NEA	MEG	Nuffield	LEAG A	LEAG B	SEG	WJEC	Alt.
sulphur	●	●		●		●		●
oxygen	●	●	●	●	●	●	●	●
halogens	●	●		●	●	●	●	●
Hydrogen	●	●	●	●	●			
Inert gases	●	●	●	●	●	●	●	●
Compounds as ionic/ molecular	●	●	●	●	●	●		●
Compounds studied in detail:								
water	●	●	●(OPT)	●	●(OPT)	●	●	●
sodium chloride	●	●		●	●	●	●	●
sodium hydroxide	●		●	●		●		●
sodium carbonate					●			●
sodium hydrogen- carbonate	●				●			●
calcium carbonate	●	●	●	●	●	●		●
ammonia	●	●	●	●	●	●		●
carbon dioxide	●	●	●	●		●		●
sulphur dioxide	●			●		●	●	●
sulphuric acid	●	●	●	●	OPT	●	●	●
Radioactive chemicals	●					●	●	●
half-life	●					●	●	●
Pharmaceutical chemicals (drugs)			OPT		OPT			

Chemical models

	NEA	MEG	Nuffield	LEAG A	LEAG B	SEG	WJEC	Alt.
Particulate theory	●	●	●	●	●	●	●	●
Kinetic theory	●	●	●	●	●	●	●	●
Acids, bases, alkalis	●	●	●	●	●	●	●	●
Neutralisation reactions represented ionically	*		OPT	*	OPT	*	*	
pH scale and indicators	●	●	●	●	●	●	●	●
Strong/weak acids & bases in terms of degree of ionisation	*							
Salts – nature of	●	●	●	●	●	●	●	●
Atomic structure as n, p, e with relative mass, charge	●	●	●	●	●	●	●	●
Arrangement of electrons in elements 1–20	●	●	OPT	●	●	●	●	●

	NEA	MEG	Nuffield	LEAG A	LEAG B	SEG	Alt.	WJEC
Periodic Table:								
position related to properties	●	●	*	●	●	●	●	●
properties related to arrangement of electrons	●	●	OPT	●	●	●	●	●
amphoteric nature of some elements	*		OPT			*	●	
Nuclear chemistry:								
isotopes	●					*	*	●
stable and unstable isotopes	●						●	●
Chemical bonding:								
ionic	●	●	●	●	●	●	●	●
covalent	●	●	●	●	●	●	●	●
metallic	●	●	●		●	●	●	●
Chemical formulae:								
ionic compounds	●	●	*	●	●	●	●	●
molecular compounds	●	●	●	●	●	●	●	●
Chemical equations:								
word equations	●	●	●	●	●	●	●	●
balanced equations used in calculations of:								
reacting masses	●	●	*	●	●	●	●	●
solutions	●	●	*				●	
gases	*	●	●	*			●	
use of state symbols					●	*	*	
ionic equations	*			*		*	*	
Relative atomic mass	●	●	*	●	●	●	●	●
Relative molecular mass	●	●	●	●	●	●	●	●
Use of relative isotopic abundance	*	●				*	*	
The mole concept	*	●	*	*	●	*	●	●
used to calculate empirical formulae	*	●	●	*			●	●
used to calculate molecular formulae	*	●	●	*			●	●
Reactivity series of metals	●	●	●	●	●	●	●	
Reactivity series of halogens	*	●	●	●	●		●	
Physical and chemical changes				●	●		●	

Chemical changes

	NEA	MEG	Nuffield	LEAG A	LEAG B	SEG	Alt.	WJEC
Reason for chemical changes	●							
Energy changes:	●	●	●	●	●	●	●	●
origin	●		*		●	●		
exothermic and endothermic	●	●	●	●	●	●	●	●
representation of	*		●				●	
calculations about	*		●					
activation energy	●					●	*	
Reduction and oxidation	●	●	●	●	●	●	●	●
in terms of O, H	●	●	●	●	●	●	●	●
in terms of electrons	*	●				*	●	
Electrochemical change:								
cells	●		●	●	OPT	●		●
electrolysis	●	●	●	●	●	●	●	●
of melts	●	●	●	●	●	●	●	●
of solutions	●	●	●	●	●	*	●	●
calculations about			*	*				
Speed of chemical change	●	●	●	●	●	●	●	●
factors affecting	●	●	●	●	●	●	●	●
explanation of factors	*	●			●	*	●	●
Reversible reactions	●	●	●		●	*	●	●
Chemical equilibrium			*				*	
Thermal decomposition	●						●	
Other types of chemical reaction							●	

Chemical resources

	NEA	MEG	Nuffield	LEAG A	LEAG B	SEG	Alt.	WJEC
Distribution of chemicals in nature (incl. air)	●	●	●		●	●	●	●
Primary extraction	●	●	OPT			●	●	●
Chemical processing – principles of	*		OPT		OPT			●
Decisions in industry			OPT	●	OPT			●
Nuclear energy	●						●	●
Chemical reactions as energy sources	●	●	●		●	●	●	●
types of chemical	●	●	●		●	●	●	●
reserves & rate of use	●	●		●	●	●	●	●

	NEA	MEG	Nuffield A	LEAG A	LEAG B	SEG	SEG Alt.	WJEC
Alternative energy sources		•		•	•	•	•	•
Chemicals as material								
sources	•	•	•	•	•	•	•	•
types of chemical	•	•	•	•	•	•	•	•
reserves & rate of use	•	•		•	•	•	•	•
addition polymerisation	•		•	•	•(OPT)	*	•	•
condensation polymerisation			•		OPT			
Recycling of chemicals	•	•			•	•	•	•

Chemical consequences

	NEA	MEG	Nuffield A	LEAG A	LEAG B	SEG	SEG Alt.	WJEC
Wealth creation	*		•		OPT			
Pollution	•	•		•	•	•	•	•
of air	•	•	•	•	•	•	•	•
of land (by solids)	•	•		•	•	•	•	•
of water	•	•	OPT	•	•(OPT)	•	•	•
control of	•	•	•		•	•	•	•
Food supply	•	•		•	•	•	•	•
fertiliser N, P, K values	•	•				•	•	•
Benefits of chemistry	•	•	OPT		OPT	•	•	
Socially harmful effects	•	•		•	•		•	•
Potential harm from chemicals	•	•		•	•	•	•	•

Chemical techniques

	NEA	MEG	Nuffield A	LEAG A	LEAG B	SEG	SEG Alt.	WJEC
Separation	•	•	•	•	•	•	•	•
Tests for purity	•	•		•	•	•	•	•
Measurements	•	•		•	•	•	•	
Identification:								
of water	•	•	•	•	•	•	•	•
of common gases	•	•	•	•		•	•	
of cations	*	•	•	•	OPT			•
of anions	•	•	•	•				•
Modern analytical chemistry			OPT		OPT			
Preparation of salts:								
insoluble	•	•		•	•			•
soluble	•	•		•	•			•

KEY POINTS FROM SECTION 3

1 *The assessment objectives in the National Criteria for Chemistry lay down the content of the GCSE examination.*

2 *The core syllabus content for any GCSE Chemistry syllabus is also given in the National Criteria, and the Examining Groups have been able to add up to half as much again to make the final syllabus.*

3 *The content of eight final GCSE Chemistry syllabuses has been summarised in a table.*

SECTION 4
GCSE chemistry examinations

We have seen how the syllabus content of GCSE chemistry has been defined, and how it is related to the National Criteria for GCSE. But what will the GCSE chemistry examinations be like?

MODES

First of all, it is important to realise that there are a number of different possible 'modes' for GCSE, depending on who devises the syllabus and who carries out the examination.

Mode 1

The examining board sets the syllabus and runs the examinations (except for parts such as coursework and practical work).

Mode 2

The school designs the syllabus but the board carries out the examinations (except coursework and practical work).

Mode 3

The school designs the syllabus and carries out the examinations ('moderated' by the board to ensure fairness).

Sometimes it is possible to mix together Mode 1 and Mode 3 aspects, and this is called a 'mixed mode' examination. Different examination modes were, of course, already common in the CSE.

GRADES

Whatever the 'mode' of the examinations, the system of grades which can be obtained is the same. It was explained earlier (page 7) that, eventually, grades will be related to specific criteria. More details of what is expected under 'criterion referencing' are given at the end of this section. But for at least the first two years of GCSE, the relationship between different grades will be based on the relationship that there was between grades in GCE 'O' level and CSE ('norm' referencing).

GCSE grades will be roughly equivalent to GCE and CSE grades as shown below.

CSE	GCSE	GCE 'O' Level
	A	A
1	B	B
	C	C
2	D	D
3	E	E
4	F	
5	G	

So in GCSE you can get grades A to G. If you do not reach the minimum standard for grade G, then you will receive no certificate.

Descriptions of what will be expected of a grade C candidate and of a grade F candidate, both under the 'norm referencing' system and eventually under 'criterion referencing', have been produced. These are set out below, and they give a fair idea of what standards have to be reached, across the four major assessment objectives for GCSE chemistry (which were explained in Section 3).

Assessment Objective	GCSE Grade C	GCSE Grade F
Experimental work	Shows a reasonable competence in practical skills, e.g. can select apparatus and perform a simple operation.	Can carry out simple practical tasks under supervision, e.g. can separate a suitable mixture by filtration.
Knowledge and recall	Shows a good knowledge of factual chemistry, e.g. can recall the chemical reactions involved in simple tests for some ions in solution.	Shows some knowledge of factual chemistry, e.g. can draw and label simple diagrams, can recall simple tests for some ions in solution.
Understanding	Shows a reasonable understanding of chemical patterns, principles and theories, e.g. can write simple balanced equations, can perform numerical calculations with guidance given on method.	Shows a limited understanding of chemical patterns, principles and theories, e.g. can write 'word' chemistry equations, can plot simple graphs in which the axes are labelled.

Application, analysis, synthesis and evaluation	Shows an awareness of the contributions and applications of chemistry to social, economic, and technological problems, e.g. can use chemical knowledge in everyday situations.	Shows some appreciation of social, economic, environmental and technological problems, e.g. can link chemical knowledge with some everyday situations.

In Section 3, it was explained how the assessment objective and the content of GCSE chemistry are related to each other. The National Criteria for chemistry define the emphasis which must be placed in the examinations on the different assessment objectives and on the different areas of content.

Assessment objectives

Experimental work	minimum	20%
Recall/knowledge	–	
Understanding	minimum	20%
Application, analysis synthesis and evaluation	minimum	20%

Recall/knowledge and Understanding: about 45%

Content

Elements and compounds	minimum	10%
Ideas, models, patterns and theories	minimum	10%
Chemistry in industry	minimum	10%
Social, economic environmental and technological application	minimum	15%
Extension to the core	maximum	$\frac{1}{3}$

Elements and compounds / Ideas, models, patterns and theories: minimum 30%

Chemistry in industry / Social, economic environmental and technological application / Extension to the core: minimum 30%

The different syllabuses of the five examination groups have slightly different figures in the categories above, but they have to be within these limits.

POSITIVE ASSESSMENT

There are other important changes associated with GCSE. One of these is the change to what has been called 'positive assessment'.

The way examinations work at the moment, it is often difficult for every student to show on paper what he or she is capable of. This is because the actual examination papers and the questions which they contain are designed in such a way that there is as big a spread as possible in the marks which are obtained.

So, often, questions are set in which the first part has to be answered correctly before the candidate has any chance of doing the next part, and so on. A very able person has no difficulty. But for the less able, the first hurdle in the question may prove to be too high. So no marks can be gained, because nothing correct has been written. But that does not always mean that the candidate did not know anything about the subject matter in the question. It is simply that no opportunity to demonstrate this knowledge was given.

The 'old' system has been labelled 'negative assessment' because it meant that you lost marks for what you did not know. The GCSE is designed so that you *gain marks for what you do know*. Assessment is 'positive assessment'.

This means that examination questions in written papers, and other forms of assessment in GCSE, have to be such that you can show what you know, what you understand and what you can do. The objective in GCSE is to let you succeed – at your own level of ability. You should be given tasks which you can do comfortably and others which will stretch you to the limit. But one person's limit is another person's 'comfortably'! So, if this is going to apply to everybody who takes GCSE, a way has to be found of making sure that the tasks which everyone faces are matched to their ability.

In the GCSE exam you will not have to pick the questions you answer from a selection of questions of varying difficulty. In examination conditions this would create too much strain. Instead, the following methods have been adopted:

1 Using different examination papers aimed at different parts of the grade range.
2 Using questions which have a number of parts which increase in difficulty within each question. Some of these may be 'comprehension' type questions.
3 Using questions to which there is no single 'correct' answer, but which can be answered in varying degrees of sophistication, depending on the level of understanding.
4 Using coursework tasks which allow individuals to show evidence of science skills at different levels by the way they respond.

DIFFERENTIATED EXAMINATION PAPERS

All the examining groups have chosen to use similar patterns of examination papers in chemistry. There will be a common paper (or papers) taken by all candidates; this will only allow grades G to C to be gained.

31

Some candidates will then do an extension paper, which will let them obtain up to grade A. How this works in detail is different from one group to another, and from one syllabus to another.

Some groups have only one common written paper, some have two. But internal assessment of practical work is always a part of the 'common' element in the examinations. So you will have one or two written papers, plus internal 'coursework' assessment (which is described in more detail below). In addition, if you are going for a grade above C, you will have one more written paper.

The tables below are a summary of the pattern of examination papers for the five groups.

1 Grades G to C

	SEG	Alt.	MEG	Nuffield	NEA	LEAG A	B	WJEC
Common Paper 1	80%	40%	40%	75%	80%	40%	40%	80% (+10% on practical)
Common Paper 2	–	49%	40%	–	–	40%	35%	–
Coursework	20%	20%	20%	25%	20%	20%	25%	10%

2 Grades G to A

	SEG	Alt.	MEG	Nuffield	NEA	LEAG A	B	WJEC
Common Paper 1	40%	20%	–	–	30%	40%	40%	40%
Common Paper 2	–	20%	–	–	–	–	–	–
Extension Paper	40%	40%	●	75%	50%	40%	35%	40% (+10% on practical)
Coursework	20%	20%	●	25%	20%	20%	25%	10%

These tables need a little explanation. In all cases, except for the LEAG syllabus (B) (Nuffield), coursework will count for 20% of total marks. In this one case, 5% of marks have been moved from the second written paper to the coursework assessment. However, overall, for the award of grades G to C, the pattern is fairly straightforward (Table 1). But the different groups have taken slightly different decisions about how the award of grades A and B will take place.

Grades A/B: MEG (both syllabuses)

You have to get a grade C on the 'common' part of the examination for your work on the extension paper to count. If you do, you can get an A or a B if your work on the extension paper is of a high enough standard. So the extension paper does not 'count' towards the overall

100%. It is looked at after all the marks have been given and grades from G to C decided on. In the Nuffield examination, 75% of the marks in deciding the award of grades A and B come from the extension paper, 25% from the coursework. In the non-Nuffield examination no percentages have been given.

Grades A/B: NEA and WJEC

The NEA and WJEC suggest that only those candidates likely to achieve A, B or C grades should take the extension paper. For those who do, marks will be added up in the *two* ways shown in the tables. Candidates will then be given the *better* of the two grades. So doing the extension paper cannot make you get a lower grade than you would have done without it.

Grades A/B: LEAG (both syllabuses)

The LEAG has a common paper, and then you have to do either a paper designed for candidates in the range G to C, or one designed for Grades D to A. It will be possible for an individual to get a grade outside these ranges if that is what their performance deserves.

Grades A/B: SEG (both syllabuses)

To be eligible for grades A and B, candidates will need to take an additional paper. This extension paper will carry equal weight to the common paper(s) for such candidates. To obtain grade A, candidates need to achieve a standard of grade A, overall and on the extension paper itself.

The types of questions in the different papers will be described in the next section.

Your teacher will guide you to enter for the combination of papers which suits you best. In doing this, they will be helped by assessments which they will be making of your work themselves. As in all the science subjects, at least 20% of the total marks must be given for practical and experimental skills. A minimum of half these marks must be for experimental and observational work which you have carried out (not necessarily in the laboratory).

COURSEWORK

'Coursework' means any work which you do during your chemistry course which is assessed for the purposes of the examination. So it could be practical work in the laboratory, project work which results in a piece of written or practical work, or a long piece of work which is assessed from time to time and which also leads to a finished product like an essay or a final piece of practical work.

Coursework will be important in GCSE chemistry because it allows candidates to show certain skills which cannot be shown during written examinations. For example, the ability to review work in hand, to evaluate and adopt the approach being used to solve a chemical problem over a period of time, can only be shown by doing coursework. Coursework also allows for positive assessment, because it allows students to examine problems in their own terms and to get as far with solving them as they are able to without help.

Your teacher will find suitable tasks for you to tackle in your coursework. These will be chosen so that you are both learning and showing your abilities as a scientist as you work. Sometimes you will be given a fairly short, simple task with a definite goal; at other times you could be posed a problem which is very wide and which will allow plenty of scope in the way it is tackled. Sometimes you will be given clear guidance as to how to carry out your work; sometimes it will all be left to you. You may be given a problem in writing, or it may come up from what you read, see or hear. The result of your work can vary in its form too. You might make something, write something or even just report in words on what you have done.

So the possibilities of coursework are many. Sometimes you might also be asked to carry out specific tasks on which you will be assessed, for instance by doing a particular experiment.

Each of the examining groups has given clear guidance to teachers on exactly how to assess GCSE chemistry coursework. The details vary from one syllabus to another, but in all cases the following is true.

1 Coursework assessments will be made during the final two years of your GCSE chemistry course.

2 Much of this will be during normal work carried out during normal lesson time, or in written work produced in lessons.

3 What will be assessed will be skills which you show, not the practical work itself. So some people in the class will be assessed on one day and some on another. You will often be working as one of a group during assessment.

4 You do not have to know when you are being assessed, but normally you will. This is up to your teacher.

5 The examiners will make sure that the marks given for coursework are fair and do not vary from school to school.

6 Very clear criteria are laid down for your teacher to use during assessment. These explain exactly what skills to look for and how to spot them. You will have to be assessed on several occasions during the two years, since skills have to be observed on more than one occasion.

To give you some idea of the kind of assessment which will be made, the MEG syllabus sets out six skills to be assessed. Each is defined in terms of three levels of achievement. One mark is given for performance at level 1 (lowest level), two for performance at level 2, and 3 for performance at level 3 (highest level). Zero is awarded if level 1 is not reached. The skills and their different levels are as follows:

	Level 1	*Level 2*	*Level 3*
A Follow instructions	Follow written instructions to perform a single practical procedure or, given careful structuring, a series of practical procedures.	Follow written or oral instructions to perform an experiment involving a number of distinct stages.	Follow branching instructions.
B Use techniques, apparatus and materials	Use 'everyday' chemical apparatus correctly and safely.	Use apparatus, techniques and quantities of reagents appropriate to the experiments being undertaken.	Use appropriate techniques and quantities competently.
C Make and record observations and measurements	Make one and, with guidance, further observations during an experiment and record them in comprehensible form. Read uniform scales to an accuracy within one numbered scale division.	Record clearly, without prompting, most visible changes in an experiment. Read scales on apparatus and instruments where the reading is between numbered scale divisions.	Record clearly and accurately a wide range of observations. Read scales accurately.

D Identify problems and plan investigations	Given a series of leading facts, perceive that a problem exists. Plan a one-stage investigation, given the problem.	Perceive a problem to be investigated in a chemical situation. Plan a multi-stage investigation to solve a problem, either given or generated as above.	Analyse a problem, and suggest a number of ways of investigating it.
E Report, interpret and evaluate observations and experimental data	Make a valid deduction from a single experimental result and from a series of results designed to lead to a clear conclusion.	Come to a conclusion with a series of results.	Come to a justified conclusion from a range of results of different type. Produce an explanation that takes account of any inconsistent results.
F Evaluate methods and suggest possible improvements	Identify a weakness in a method when told that it has one, and suggest a modification.	Detect, without prompting, a weakness in a particular method and, suggest appropriate modifications.	Evaluate a method in the light of results obtained and, if appropriate, suggest alternative methods which would give improved results.

Illustrations of some of these skills and levels are given here.

Skill B   *Use techniques, apparatus and materials*

Level 1   Can use the apparatus for common chemical techniques such as filtering and heating a solid safely.

Level 2   Besides being able to use apparatus of the correct type and scale for a wide range of reagents, e.g. to test solubility or to find the effect of heat on a substance, is able to see the dangers inherent in certain ways of working – e.g. when heating a liquid in a tube takes suitable safety precautions such as pointing it away from others.

Level 3   Can carry out unaided more complex operations such as distilling a flammable liquid.

Skill D   *Identify problems and plan investigations*

Level 1   Can devise a test to see which of four black powders is the best catalyst for the decomposition of hydrogen peroxide. For example, the student adds hydrogen peroxide to each powder in turn and sees which fizzes the most.

Level 2   Can devise an experiment to see if a black powder is a catalyst, i.e. speeds up the reaction and doesn't appear to be consumed. For example, the student mixes hydrogen peroxide with each powder in turn and attempts to control the quantities used.

Level 3   Can devise an experiment to show that a substance is a catalyst by observing its effect on reaction rate and by proving by weighing that it isn't consumed, and also keeping the quantity of hydrogen peroxide constant.

Skill E   *Report, interpret and evaluate observations and experimental data*

Level 1   Given the help of data sheets, can identify a gas or distinguish between acid and alkali from an appropriate test.
Given a set of soluble metal oxides can decide that these metal oxides are basic.

Level 2   From the results of shaking metal oxides with water and indicator solution can decide that metal oxides are basic (alkaline) even though some of the tests show no change in the colour of the indicator.

Level 3   From shaking metal oxides with water, acids and alkalis can conclude that metal oxides are basic and that some are soluble and are, therefore, alkalis. If hydroxides were used, can also arrive at a conclusion regarding amphoteric oxides.

In another syllabus, the LEAG syllabus B (Nuffield), there are six criteria for assessment:

1	Ability to organise practical work and follow instructions	8 marks
2	Manipulative skills	8 marks
3	Accuracy of observations and measurements	8 marks
4	Presentation of experimental results and conclusions	8 marks
5	Ability to design and plan experiments	8 marks
6	Appreciation of the social, industrial and environmental aspects of the chosen option	12 marks

There will be a minimum of five practical assessments, chosen in such a way that at least two are on the options work and each of the abilities 1 to 5 is assessed on at least two separate occasions. There must also be at least three other assessments of the options work with respect to ability 6. These must include:

(i)   a piece of writing;
(ii)   a written test;
(iii)   oral work.

Where there are more than two assessments of each of the abilities 1 to 5, the best two marks in each case will count. Similarly, the best three assessments for ability 6 will count. In each case, the maximum mark is 4. So the total is out of 52 ($5 \times 2 \times 4$) + ($1 \times 3 \times 4$)). The mark scheme which must be used for assessing the various criteria is as follows:

1   Ability to organise practical work and follow instructions

Understands the aim of the experiment and is able to organise work in a safe and logical way. Follows oral and written instructions well for multiple and complex tasks without requiring assistance.	4 marks
Understands the aim of the experiment and works well and safely with little assistance. Can follow most oral and written instructions without help.	3 marks
Sometimes needs help to understand the aim of the experiment and to work safely and accurately. Follows oral and written instructions for a limited range of tasks.	2 marks
Often needs a lot of help to understand the aim of the experiment and to organise the work. Able to follow written and oral instructions concerning a single task.	1 mark
Shows no understanding of the aim of the experiment and is unable to organise or follow instructions even with help.	0 marks

2   Manipulative skills

Sets up apparatus and handles chemicals safely and accurately. Performs the experiment without assistance.	4 marks
Sets up and uses apparatus competently, but occasionally needs assistance in matters of detail. Handles chemicals safely.	3 marks
Sets up apparatus and handles chemicals satisfactorily but sometimes needs direction in matters of technique.	2 marks
Demonstrates skills in the setting up of apparatus and use of chemicals but needs help and direction.	1 mark
Makes no manipulative contribution to the experiment.	0 marks

3 *Accuracy of observations and measurement*

Observes, measures and records accurately and with
due care.   4 marks

Observes, measures and records most of what is required
by the experiment, generally with suitable accuracy.   3 marks

Observes, measures and records some of what is required
by the experiment with a fair degree of accuracy.   2 marks

Makes and records one of the observations or
measurements required.   .   1 mark

No observations or measurements recorded.   0 marks

4 *Ability to present experimental results clearly and draw
conclusions from them*

Results presented in a logical manner, calculations correct.
Well drawn conclusions.   4 marks

Results well presented and calculations correct. Conclusions
correct but sometimes lacking insight or originality.   3 marks

Results reasonably well presented, calculations contain
minor errors. Conclusions not fully comprehensive.   2 marks

Able to present results but needs assistance with
interpretation and calculations.   1 mark

No results presented. No conclusions drawn.   0 marks

5 *Ability to design and plan experiments*

Understands the aims of the practical work and can
independently and competently plan and organise the
necessary work without assistance. Can also adapt the
planned work to cope with a changing or developing
situation.   4 marks

Understands the basic aims of the practical work and can
plan and organise the work without assistance. May need
guidance in adapting the planned work to changing
circumstances.   3 marks

Understands the basic aims of the experiment but sometimes needs assistance in planning and organising the work
efficiently. Needs assistance if the work has to be
adapted to changed circumstances.   2 marks

Shows some understanding of the aims of the experiment
but requires assistance to plan and design the work.   1 mark

Is unable to understand the aims of the work or to
formulate plans for efficient and safe working.   0 marks

6 *Appreciation of the social, industrial and environmental aspects of the chosen options*

Is fully aware of the social, industrial and environmental implications of the chosen option. Is able to evaluate the relevance and accuracy of reports in the media and to defend a point of view in discussion.   4 marks

Is aware of the implications of the chosen option and makes a good contribution to discussion using material from a variety of sources. Some errors of judgement with respect to the relevance of material.   3 marks

Is aware that social, industrial and environmental issues are important in relation to the study of the chosen option but needs help in selecting material and evaluating its importance. Finds it difficult to defend a point of view against detailed questioning.   2 marks

Is able to list facts relating to social, industrial and environmental issues. Needs support in discussing and evaluating their importance.   1 mark

Is unable to see the social, industrial and environmental relevance of the option work or to contribute to discussion   0 marks

Each of the other GCSE chemistry syllabuses contains similar criteria and rules for the assessment of coursework by teachers.

CRITERION REFERENCING

We have said that GCSE grades will eventually be linked to a list of 'can do's', but that for at least the first two years of GCSE this will not be the case. This is because it will take time to define the criteria for grades and then test them so that everyone is satisfied by their accuracy. In the meantime, at least the assessment of coursework will be according to criteria, as we have just seen.

But what will 'criterion-referencing' of GCSE chemistry grades mean, in practice? For the moment we only know the draft proposals for criterion referencing. So what follows may be changed to a greater or lesser extent in the system which eventually comes into being.

DOMAINS

It is being suggested that chemistry should be divided up into three areas or 'domains'.

Domain A Knowledge with understanding

Recall and understanding of knowledge in relation to
1   language: terms, symbols, quantities and units;
2   facts, phenomena, concepts, principles, patterns, models and theories;
3   the techniques, procedures and principles of safe laboratory work.

Domain B Handling information and solving problems

The ability, using oral, written, symbolic, graphic and numerical material, to
4   select and present information from a variety of sources;
5   translate information from one form to another;
6   use information to identify patterns, report trends and draw inferences;
7   present reasoned explanations for phenomena, patterns and relationships;
8   propose hypotheses and make predictions;
9   solve problems, including some of a quantitative nature.

Domain C Experimental skills and investigations

The ability in relation to laboratory or field work to
10   identify problems and plan investigations;
11   organise and conduct investigations;
12   interpret, evaluate and report upon observations and experimental data;
13   evaluate methods and suggest improvements;
and, in the course of such work to
14   follow instructions, select and use techniques, apparatus and materials;
15   make and record observations, measurements and estimates.

The applications of chemistry and its social, economic and environmental implications should be an integral part of the content assessed via the three domains. Domain C would probably be assessed by teachers, and so might some aspects of the other domains.

From domain performance to grades

It is being suggested that performance in each domain should contribute equally to the overall grade for the subject. In each domain, a grade from a to g would be possible. These would be arrived at by adding up scores for assessments on the different parts of each domain.

The grade (a–g) in each domain would be translated into a number from 7 to 1.

a	b	c	d	e	f	g
7	6	5	4	3	2	1

So the maximum score that could be obtained by adding together the score on each domain is 21. Overall grades would be awarded according to a scale.

Overall grade	A	B	C	D	E	F	G
Sum of domain scores (minimum necessary)	20	17	14	11	8	5	2

There is one more complication. To get a particular grade, two of the three domain scores must be at that level at least. So to obtain an overall C, you need two c's or better, and so on. Some examples are given below.

	Domain scores	Sum	Overall Grade	Reason
Candidate 1	a b c	7 + 6 + 5 = 18	B	Min. 17 and two b's or better
Candidate 2	c a d	5 + 7 + 4 = 16	C	Min. 14 and two c's or better
Candidate 3	e b d	3 + 6 + 4 = 13	D	Min. 11 and two d's or better
Candidate 4	d e a	4 + 3 + 7 = 14	D	Min. 14 achieved, but only two d's or better
Candidate 5	c a g	5 + 7 + 1 = 13	D	Min. 11 and two domains at better than d (Min. 14 for overall C not achieved)
Candidate 6	a a b	7 + 7 + 6 = 20	A	Min. 20 and two a's

However, there are technical difficulties associated with combining scores in this way, and it is possible that the suggestions above will have to be revised.

Assessing domain performance

In the same way that the different examination groups have given illustrations of performance on coursework skills in their syllabuses for the 1988 examination, possible illustrations of performance at different levels in the proposed domains for criterion referenced examinations have been worked out. These are the 'can do's' that make up the criterion referencing. Some examples of the abilities that will have to be shown in the different domains for different levels of performance are set out below.

Domain A (Knowledge with understanding)

Level 1 (low)

Being able to explain terms like 'saturated solution'.

Being able to use correct units such as $^\circ$C for temperature, g for mass.

Being able to identify elements and simple compounds from their symbols.

Being able to write word equations for reactions such as metal and acid.

Knowing that fractions can be obtained from crude oil.

Understanding that oxidation is gain of oxygen and reduction is loss of oxygen in situations like respiration, burning and rusting and reduction of metal oxides.

Being able to describe how to remove an insoluble solid from a liquid by filtration.

Level 2 (intermediate)

Being able to use the correct chemical term in the right context.

Being able to describe the physical events represented by equations in symbols with state symbols.

Being able to to write equations in symbols which involve elements and simple compounds and which can be balanced using numbers no higher than 2.

Knowing what property of liquids enables them to be separated by fractional distillation.

Knowing that redox reactions involve both oxygen and hydrogen loss and gain and that these two changes always happen together.

Being able to describe how to make a clean, dry sample of an insoluble salt.

Level 3 (high)

Being able to use chemical terminology correctly and realising that some terms can have a different meaning in a non-chemical context.

Given a concentration in g/dm^3, calculating the mass dissolved in $300\,cm^3$.

Being able to describe how fractional distillation works in terms of the evaporation and condensation of liquids of different boiling point.

Knowing that redox reactions can be described in terms of loss and gain of electrons.

Being able to decide on the correct procedure to prepare a particular salt given the necessary information about its properties.

Domain B (Handling information and solving problems)

Level 1 (low)

Being able to select information such as a melting point from a table of data.

Recognising from data that metals always go to the negative electrode in electrolysis.

Being able to look for evidence of a correlation between fluoride content of water and the incidence of dental decay.

Being able to design and describe an experiment to compare the solubility in water of two brands of aspirin.

Level 2 (intermediate)

Being able to select information on the amounts of the five most abundant elements in the earth's crust and present it in a form such as a bar or pie chart.

Being able to find recurring patterns going across successive Periods of the Periodic Table.

Being able to relate reactivity of elements to ease of loss or gain of electrons. Given three sites for an aluminium smelter, being able to deduce which is best on the basis of the environmental effects, cost effectiveness and transport availability.

Level 3 (high)

Being able to collate information from given sources to deduce some scientific causes of the world food problem.

Being able to relate changes in reactivity in a group of elements in the Periodic Table to electron arrangements and atomic radii.

Being able to put forward explanations for different e.m.f. values for cells of different pairs of elements.

By analysis of data of trace elements in the soil, in the livers of animals and of the geology of the area, to be able to decide on the possible reasons for ill-health in cattle and suggest a remedy.

Domain C (Experimental skills and investigations)

Level 1 (low)

Being able to devise a test to investigate the flammability of a material.

Being able to investigate which of a number of salts gives off water when heated.

Given the help of data sheets, being able to identify an unknown gas.

Being able to read scales on a balance, a thermometer, a measuring cylinder or a stop-clock to the nearest division.

Level 2 (intermediate)

Being able to devise an experiment to see if a black powder is a catalyst.

Being able to investigate, without the help of structured prompts, what happens when hydrated copper(II) sulphate is heated.

Being able to identify several ions in a mixture.

Being able to read any scale likely to be encountered in chemistry when reading is between marked divisions.

Level 3 (high)

Being able to devise an experiment to show a substance is a catalyst by its effect on reaction rate and by proving that it is not used up.

Being able to carry out a complete investigation on being asked to discover what happens when hydrated cobalt chloride is heated.

Being able to carry out investigation of problems involving analyses not met before and where results may appear to be confusing.

Being able to read all scales encountered as accurately as the scale permits.

However, for those taking GCSE chemistry examinations in 1988 and 1989, criterion referencing and the use of domains will not apply. Your grades will be arrived at by the methods described earlier in this section (see particularly the section about differentiated examination papers on p.31).

But what types of questions will be in these papers? Section 5 gives a large number of examples, most of which are 'sample' questions from the different GCSE chemistry syllabuses.

KEY POINTS FROM SECTION 4

1 GCSE chemistry examinations can be in one of three 'modes'.

2 The system of grades will have a correspondence with the system of grades for GCE 'O' level and CSE.

3 The performance expected of candidates who will obtain grades C and grades F have been described in words, across the four major assessment objectives for GCSE chemistry.

4 *The relative emphasis in the examinations of the four assessment objectives, and of different aspects of the content of GCSE chemistry, have been defined.*

5 *Assessment in GCSE chemistry will be 'positive' assessment.*

6 *To allow for positive assessment, each examining group has devised its own set of 'differentiated' examination papers. Candidates aiming at grades above C will, in each case, need to take an 'extension' paper.*

7 *The assessment of coursework by teachers will also make an important contribution to positive assessment.*

8 *When criterion referencing is agreed, a different system, linked to definitions of performance in various 'domains' of chemistry, will be used to award final grades.*

SECTION 5
Sample GCSE chemistry questions

The syllabuses from the five GCSE examining groups state the different types of question which they will use in examination papers.

TYPES OF QUESTION

The different types of question are as follows.

Multiple-choice questions

These questions are used to test a wide range of skills and knowledge in a short space of time. A question is followed by a list of alternatives (usually five), one of which is the best answer. You answer by choosing the best alternative, which will correspond to a letter A–E. In many cases you will then have to mark an answer sheet, which will be read by a machine.

A typical multiple-choice question is the following:

An atom or group of atoms possessing an electric charge is known as

    A   an ion
    B   a molecule
    C   a neutron
    D   an electron
    E   an electrode

(*Answer:* A).   *(LEAG, syllabus A)*

Matching-pairs questions

These are very similar to multiple-choice questions. The difference is that the same set of alternative answers is used for a group of questions. The following example shows how this is done.

The group of questions over the page consists of five possible answers

followed by a list of numbered questions. For each question select the best answer. Each answer may be used once, more than once, or not at all.

Questions 1-4 concern the following practical methods:

A chromatography
B crystallization
C distillation
D electrolysis
E filtration

Choose, from A to E, the method which would be used to
1 isolate nitrogren from liquid air C
2 separate coloured substances in a sample of coloured soft drink A
3 separate petrol from crude oil C E
4 separate a drug which has been precipitated from a solution. E

(*Answers 1* C. *2* A *3* C *4* E)   (*LEAG, syllabus A*)

Short-answer questions

These are questions to which you have to provide the answer yourself, but this only needs to be very simple – a word, a sentence or a simple diagram or calculation. The following are some examples:

1 The element used to kill harmful bacteria in water is . . . .
   (*Answer:* chlorine)   (*NEA, syllabus A*)

2 Give the name or formula of a gas present in polluted air which can cause damage to buildings.
   (*Answer:* sulphur dioxide/SO_2)   (*NEA, syllabus A*)

3 Complete the following word equation
   magnesium + oxygen → . . . .
   (*Answer:* magnesium oxide)   (*NEA, syllabus A*)

(The exam paper will usually give dotted lines for your answer, but we have omitted those in this book.)

Structured questions

These are questions which contain several parts which are linked together, usually around a common idea. You have to answer each part, and it will be clear from the question whether a word, a sentence or a diagram is needed. The answers usually have to be fuller (that is, more detailed) than those for short-answer questions, and overall the questions are more difficult. Often, the parts of the question get harder as you work through it.

An example is the following:

The following diagram is a simple outline of a blast furnace:

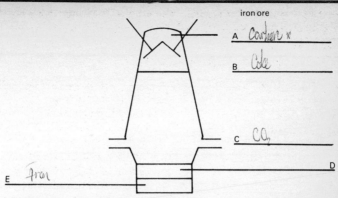

iron ore

A Carbon ✗

B Coke

C CO₂

D

E Iron

(a) Complete the labelling of the diagram by writing the names of the raw materials **A**, **B** and **C**, and the names of the products **D** and **E** in the spaces provided. **(5 marks)**

(*Answers: A* limestone, *B* coke, *C* air, *D* slag, *E* iron)

(b) Name the type of chemical reaction involved when iron ore is converted to iron. **(1 mark)**

(*Answer:* reduction).

(c) Complete the equation for the conversion of iron ore to iron.

$Fe_2O_3 + 3CO \rightarrow$ .... Fe_2 ..... + .. $3CO_2$ ..... **(2 marks)**

(*Answer:* $2Fe + 3CO_2$)

(d) Explain why aluminium is not extracted from its ore by a similar process to that used for iron. **(2 marks)**

(*Answer:* Aluminium is a more reactive metal than iron. It is also more reactive than carbon, which is more reactive than iron. So carbon (coke) is reactive enough to reduce iron ore to iron, but not reactive enough to reduce aluminium ore to aluminium.)

(e) Iron reacts with chlorine according to the equation:

$$2Fe + 3Cl_2 \rightarrow 2FeCl_3$$

What is the relative molecular mass of iron(III) chloride, $FeCl_3$?

$$(Fe = 56, Cl = 35.5)$$ **(1 mark)**

(*Answer:*   Relative molecular mass of $FeCl_3$

       $= (1 \times 56) + (3 \times 35.5)$

       $= 56 + 106.5$

       $= 162.5$.)

(f) **How many grams of iron would be required to make 16.25g of iron(III) chloride?** (2 marks)

    (Answer: $2Fe + 3Cl_2 \rightarrow 2FeCl_3$

                     $2 \times 56g \rightarrow 2 \times 162.5g$

                     $\therefore 56g \rightarrow 162.5g$

                     $\therefore 5.6g \rightarrow 16.25g$

                 Answer 5.6g

(g) **'Iron' tablets are sold at chemists' shops. Barium chloride solution can be used to show whether the iron is present as iron(II) sulphate.**

    (i)   Observation if iron(II) chloride is present (1 mark)

    (Answer: **No** precipitate.)

    ***(ii)* Observation if iron(II) sulphate is present** (1 mark)

    (Answer: White precipitate.)

                                         (NEA, syllabus A)

Data-response questions

A data-response question is one in which you are given some information to start with. You might then have to change this information into another form, or use it to find or work out the answer to a specific question. A data-response question might be a multiple-choice question like the following:

The Haber process produces different amounts of ammonia at different temperatures, as shown in the table below.

Temperature in °C	kg of ammonia produced	Production time
250	1100	5 hours
300	700	3 hours
350	300	1 hour
400	120	25 mins
450	50	15 mins

The temperature at which ammonia will be produced most quickly is:

A   **250°C**
B   **300°C**
C   **350°C**
D   **400°C**
E   **450°C**

(Answer: C)

                                       (LEAG, syllabus B)

Quite often, a data-response question will be a structured question:

Potassium chloride is the chemical name for an important fertiliser called 'potash'. A chemical company is trying to get potash from a mine near Whitby in Yorkshire. Unfortunately the potash is mixed with rock salt. The graph below will help you to understand one way in which potash and rock salt can be separated.

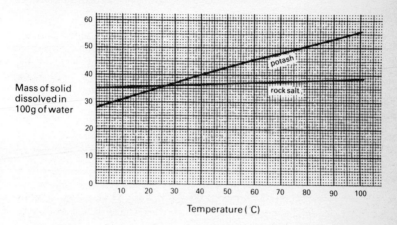

Mass of solid dissolved in 100g of water

Temperature (°C)

(a) Use the graph to find the solubility of potash and rock salt at 100°C and 20°C

Solubility at:	100°C	20°C
Potash		
Rock Salt		

(b) Suggest a method that could be used to separate rock salt from potash.

(NEA, syllabus A)

Data-response questions are used to test for higher level skills of information handling, and so some candidates will find them difficult.

In some cases, the 'data' may take the form of a passage of writing, and the question is then similar to a 'comprehension' question.

Free-response questions

Where no structure for your answer is given in the question, you have to provide that structure yourself. Free-response (or 'essay-type') questions allow scope for you to show what you know and understand about a particular part of chemistry. You will usually be asked to provide a description, an explanation or a commentary.

An example is the following:

Discuss the manufacture and importance of sulphuric acid. Your answer should include reference to the chemistry of the process, the factors affecting the siting of a plant, problems associated with storage and transport, and the economic importance and uses of sulphuric acid.

(LEAG, syllabus A)

Obviously, there is no single answer to this question, and different candidates will be able to answer it at different levels of sophistication. So free-response questions not only help provide opportunities for positive assessment, but they also allow some of the higher level skills described in Section 4 of this book to be shown. Free-response questions will usually only be used in 'extension' papers, designed for the award of grades A and B.

PATTERNS OF QUESTION TYPES

The different examining groups have stated the types of question which they will use in their examination papers. Before looking at the table below, you will find it helpful to look back to page 32 where the pattern of examination papers is described.

Southern Examining Group

Common Paper   12 short answer and 6 structured questions (2 hours)
Extension Paper   Approximately 6 structured questions, some of which contain a free-response part (1½ hours)

Southern Examining Group (Alternative) (Nuffield)

Common Paper 1 50 multiple-choice/matching-pairs questions (1 hour)
Common Paper 2 Structured questions (1 hour)
Extension Paper Structured and longer questions, one of which may be a 'comprehension' question (1¼ hours)

Midland Examining Group

Common Paper 1 50 multiple-choice questions (1 hour)
Common Paper 2 Short-answer and structured questions (1 hour)
Extension Paper Structured questions and free-response questions (choice of 2 from 3) (1¼ hours)

Midland Examining Group (Nuffield)

Common Paper 1 Short-answer and structured questions (1½ hours)
Extension Paper Structured questions and free-response questions (1½ hours)

Northern Examining Association

Common Paper   Multiple-choice, matching-pairs, short-answer and structured questions (including opportunity for free response) (2 hours)

Extension Paper   Structured and free-response questions (1½ hours)

London and East Anglian Group (Syllabus A)

Common Paper 1 50 multiple-choice and matching-pairs questions (1 hour)

Common Paper 2 Structured questions (2 hours)

Extension Paper   Structured questions and longer questions including free-response (choice of 3 from 5) (2 hours)

London and East Anglian Group (Syllabus B) (Nuffield)

Common Paper 1 50 multiple-choice and matching-pairs questions (1 hour)

Common Paper 2 Structured questions (2 hours)

Extension Paper   Structured questions and longer questions, one of which will be a 'comprehension' question (2 hours)

Welsh Joint Education Committee

Common Paper   Multiple-choice, short-answer and structured questions (including opportunity for free response) (2 hours)

Extension Paper   Structured and free-response questions (2 hours)

SAMPLE QUESTIONS

The questions which follow are arranged under the headings used to describe the content of the different GCSE chemistry syllabuses at the end of Section 3 of this book.

Chemical substances

Multiple-choice questions

1 Which element, when burned in air, forms an oxide which is used in the manufacture of an important industrial acid?

    A   calcium

    B   sulphur ✓

    C   copper

    D   nitrogen

    E   iron

(LEAG, syllabus A)

2 Using the apparatus shown below, it is possible to collect a sample of nitrogen.

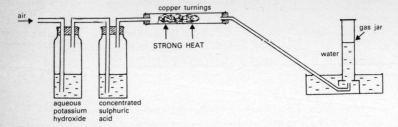

In addition to nitrogen the gas jar would also contain

A noble gases only
B hydrogen only ✓
C water vapour and noble gases
D hydrogen and noble gases
E hydrogen and water vapour

(LEAG, syllabus B)

3 Which of the following properties of metals depends most on the size of its crystals?

A colour
B density ✓
C melting point
D strength

(SEG, Alt)

4 Aluminium is obtained industrially by

A reaction of aluminium oxide with carbon in a blast furnace
B reaction of aluminium oxide with carbon monoxide in a blast furnace
C electrolysis using aluminium chloride
D electrolysis using aluminium sulphate ✓
E electrolysis using aluminium oxide

(LEAG, syllabus A)

5 A substance has the following properties:

Its solution in water conducts electricity.
It becomes white when heated but gives a coloured solution in water.
There is no evolution of gas when it is added to aqueous sodium carbonate.

The substance could be a

A   metallic element
B   non-metallic element
C   solid acid ✓
D   non-electrolyte
E   hydrated salt

(LEAG, syllabus B)

Matching-pairs questions

1 and *2*   From the list *A* to *E* below

A   iron
B   copper
C   sodium
D   zinc
E   aluminium

choose the metal which is

1   dug out of the ground in the mineral 'bauxite';   D
2   used for making objects which have to be both strong and light (such as aeroplanes).   E

3, *4* and *5* concern the properties *A* to *E* of a range of substances.

Electrical conductivity (of the pure substance) at room temperature	Solubility in water	Properties of the solution in water
A non-conductor	soluble	a neutral solution which conducts electricity
B non-conductor	soluble	a neutral solution which does NOT conduct electricity
C non-conductor	insoluble	—
D conductor	insoluble	—
E non-conductor	soluble	an alkaline solution which conducts electricity

Select, from *A* to *E*, the appropriate set of properties for

3   ammonia; B
4   copper; D
5   sodium hydroxide. A

(LEAG, syllabus A)

Short-answer questions

1 Use the diagram of the Carbon Cycle below for this question.

THE MAIN STEPS OF THE CARBON CYCLE

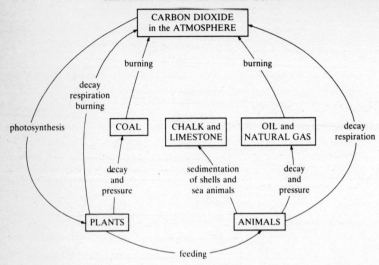

(a) What process provides plants with the carbon compounds they need? (1 mark)

(b) What substance other than carbon dioxide is used in the process? (1 mark)

(c) Give one difference between the formation of coal and the formation of oil. (1 mark)

(SEG)

(SEG)

2 What tests could you do to tell the difference between the following substances? In each case, say what you would do and what you would expect to happen.

(a) copper(II) oxide and carbon (2 marks)

(b) magnesium and iron (2 marks)

(SEG)

Questions 3 and 4

Complete these sentences by filling in the blank spaces.

3 The element used to kill harmful bacteria in drinking water is . . . . . .

4 Compounds containing nitrogen which are present in all plants and animals are called . . . .

(NEA, syllabus A)

5 The percentages of the main gases in air are shown in the table.

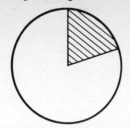

Gas	Percentage
argon	1%
nitrogen	78%
oxygen	20%

Which of the gases is shaded in the pie chart?

(NEA, syllabus B)

Structured questions

1 The diagram shows apparatus which can be used to find the composition of the air. 100cm^3 of air were placed in syringe A with syringe B empty. The copper was heated strongly and the air was passed to and from syringes A and B over the hot copper and finally returned to syringe A.

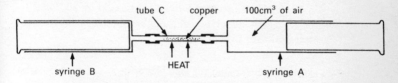

(a) (i) Which gas does copper remove from the air?
   (ii) Name the compound that is formed.
   (iii) Describe the colour change you would observe during the reaction.
   (iv) Which would be the most abundant gas in the mixture remaining in syringe A at the end of the experiment?

   (4 marks)

(b) The gas involved in the reaction is also used up during breathing.

   (i) Describe in chemical terms another process which would result in this gas being removed from the air.
   (ii) What volume of gas would be present in a 100cm^3 sample of air?
   (iii) Describe how you would test for the presence of this gas and state the result you would expect   (5 marks)

Total 9 marks

(LEAG, syllabus A)

2 This question concerns sulphuric acid (H_2SO_4) and its manufacture by the contact process.

   The starting materials used in the contact process are sulphur dioxide and oxygen. The sulphur dioxide is obtained from a variety of sources:

(i) by burning sulphur

$$S(s) + O_2(g) \rightarrow SO_2(g);$$

(ii) by burning ores which contain sulphur – iron pyrites (FeS_2) and zinc blende (ZnS) are commonly used;

(iii) by burning the hydrogen sulphide which occurs in some natural gas

$$2H_2S(g) + 2O_2(g) \rightarrow 2SO_2(g) + 2H_2(g).$$

The sulphur dioxide is dried, purified and mixed with pure, dry air. The mixture is heated to about 450°C and then passed into a converter containing a catalyst (either vanadium(V) oxide or platinum). The sulphur dioxide is oxidised by the oxygen to sulphur trioxide.

$$2SO_2(g) + O_2(g) \rightleftharpoons 2SO_3(g)$$

Sulphur trioxide can be converted into sulphuric acid by adding it to water. However, direct dissolving of sulphur trioxide in water produces practical problems in industry.

(a) Name two sources of sulphur dioxide. (2 marks)

(b) What is the chemical name for zinc blende? (1 mark)

(c) Explain what is meant by 'The sulphur dioxide is oxidised' (1 mark)

(d) (i) In the equation $2SO_2(g) + O_2(g) \rightleftharpoons 2SO_3(g)$, what does the symbol $\rightleftharpoons$ show?

(ii) Where does the oxygen come from in this reaction? (2 marks)

(e) The catalyst in the converter is expensive and can be easily ruined.
(i) Why is the high cost worthwhile?
(ii) What precaution is taken to protect the catalyst? (2 marks)

(f) Explain why the escape of sulphur dioxide from a factory producing sulphuric acid is unwise for (i) economic and (ii) environmental reasons. (4 marks)

(g) Write word and balanced symbol equations for the reaction that takes place when sulphur trioxide is added to water.

Word equation; ....

Symbolic equation: .... (3 marks)

Total 15 marks
(LEAG, syllabus B)

3 Read the passage below and answer the questions which follow.

Carbon Many of the things we use contain carbon, for instance glue, wool, rubber, leather and paper. Chemists call these substances organic. The element carbon, in the form of charcoal, was one of the first known elements. The Bible refers to charcoal or coal as a fuel. Prehistoric people used charcoal for drawing, as we use graphite today.

Sulphur This yellow, powdery element is found in Italy. People soon discovered that it would catch fire and burn quickly with a blue flame giving off a choking gas. Sulphur was often called 'brimstone'. In modern times the chief use for sulphur has been for making sulphuric acid. This chemical is of major importance in making ammonium sulphate. In England sulphur is found combined with calcium and oxygen as gypsum.

Copper This metal has been known for thousands of years and has been found uncombined in natural deposits. Copper forms many important alloys known today. Lumps of rock containing copper ore produce copper when placed in a hot fire. The metal would be molten since it melts at only about 1000°C.

(a) Explain the meaning of the following words in the passage:
  (i) 'organic';
  (ii) 'fuel';
  (iii) 'element'. (5 marks)
(b) (i) What other elements besides sulphur are present in sulphuric acid?
  (ii) What is the choking gas given off when sulphur burns?
  (4 marks)
(c) Give a use for ammonium sulphate. (1 mark)
(d) Deduce the chemical name for gypsum from the information given in the passage. (1 mark)
(e) (i) Name one other metal besides copper which is found in native deposits.
  (ii) Explain why you would NOT expect to find magnesium in native deposits. (2 marks)
(f) Give one use for copper, explaining why it is particularly suitable for this purpose. (2 marks)

Total 15 marks
(LEAG, syllabus A)

4 Carbon dioxide can be prepared by adding acid to calcium carbonate.

(a) (i) Name the salt produced by the reaction.
   (ii) What else is produced by the reaction, besides the salt and carbon dioxide? (2 marks)

(b) When a gas jar containing carbon dioxide is upturned over a burning splint, the flame goes out.

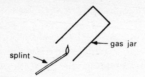

What two properties of carbon dioxide does this illustrate?

(i) . . . .

(ii) . . . .

(iii) What piece of equipment used widely in everyday life makes use of these properties? (3 marks)

(c) If a piece of magnesium is burned in a gas jar of carbon dioxide, a white powder and particles of a black solid are formed.

(i) What is the black solid?
(ii) What is the white powder?
(iii) Write a word equation for the reaction in (c). (3 marks)

Total 8 marks
(LEAG, syllabus A)

5 This question concerns the properties of the elements in one period of the Periodic Table and some of their compounds. Use the following data to answer the questions.

	Sodium	Magnesium	Aluminium	Silicon	Phosphorus	Sulphur	Chlorine	Argon
Melting point of element/°C	98	650	659	1410	44	119	−101	−190
Density at room temperature/ g cm^{-3}	0.97	1.74	2.70	2.42	1.83	2.07	0.00296	0.0017
Relative atomic mass	23	24	27	28	31	32	35.5	40
Atomic number	11	12	13	14	15	16	17	18
Formula of chloride	NaCl	MgCl$_2$	AlCl$_3$	SiCl$_4$	PCl$_3$	S$_2$Cl$_2$	Cl$_2$	−
Melting point of chloride/°C	801	708	−	−70	−92	−80	−101	−

(a) Phosphorus has two common allotropes. Mark, with a cross, two boxes in the table where you would expect to find additional data. (1 mark)

(b) (i) Which non-metallic element has a giant structure of atoms?

(ii) Which piece of information did you use to help you make your decision? (2 marks)

(c) Which elements in the period have small molecules consisting of more than one atom? (2 marks)

(d) State the names of TWO elements which form positive ions. (1 mark)

(e) (i) What is the probable type of structure of silicon(IV) chloride?

(ii) What is the relative molecular mass of silicon(IV) chloride?

(iii) Silicon(IV) chloride reacts with water to form solid silicon(IV) oxide, SiO_2, and hydrogen chloride solution. Write a balanced equation, including state symbols, for this reaction. (4 marks)

Total 10 marks
(NEA, syllabus B)

Free-response questions

1 Discuss the manufacture and importance of sulphuric acid. Your answer should include reference to the chemistry of the process, the factors affecting the siting of the plant, problems associated with storage and transport, and the economic importance and uses of sulphuric acid.

(LEAG, syllabus A)

2 Explain why the metal iron is so important to us in modern life. You should include what you know about the properties of iron that make it so useful and the kinds of things which can be made from it, where we get iron from and the process involved, and the different materials that can be made starting from pure iron.

Specimen answers are given on pages 93–5.

Chemical models

Multiple-choice questions

1 The following metals are arranged in order of their reactivity.
magnesium (most reactive)
zinc
iron
copper

Between which of the following pairs of substances (listed over the page) will a reaction occur?

A copper and zinc sulphate
B magnesium and copper(II) sulphate
C copper and iron(II) sulphate
D iron and zinc sulphate
E zinc and magnesium sulphate

(LEAG, syllabus B)

2 If fine pollen grains on the surface of water are examined under a microcope, it will be seen that the pollen grains are in random motion, frequently changing direction. The movement is most likely to be due to

A air draughts blowing on the water
B chemical reaction between the pollen and the water
C attraction and repulsion between charged particles
D collision between water molecules and pollen grains
E electrolysis of pollen grains

(LEAG, syllabus A)

3 An atom of manganese has an atomic number of 25 and a mass number of 55. How many neutrons are contained in this atom of manganese?

A 5
B 25
C 30
D 55
E 80

(LEAG, syllabus A)

4 It is found that 2.8g of iron displaces 10.8g of silver from a silver nitrate solution. The ratio of the number of reacting particles of iron to silver is (Relative atomic masses: Fe = 56, Ag = 108)

A 1:2
B 2:1
C 1:1
D 3:1
E 2:3

(LEAG, syllabus A)

5 Ethanol can be made by fermenting glucose ($C_6H_{12}O_6$) as described in the equation below.

$$C_6H_{12}O_6(aq) \xrightarrow{\text{yeast}} 2CH_3OH(aq) + 2CO_2(g)$$

The mass of glucose needed to make 2 moles of ethanol is (Relative atomic masses: C = 12, H = 1, O = 16)

A	4g
B	88g
C	92g
D	180g
E	360g

(LEAG, syllabus B)

Matching-pairs questions

Questions 1–5 concern the diagram below, which shows part of the Periodic Table divided into five sections A, B, C, D and E.

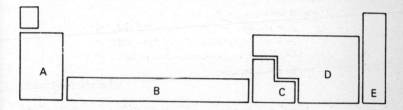

Select from A to E, the section in which you would find

1 a metal which reacts violently with water, forming hydrogen
2 an element which forms no compounds
3 metals which form a wide range of coloured compounds
4 the element with the following arrangement of electrons: 2.8.2
5 the element which is found in the ground as a yellow solid, and whose oxide reacts with water to form an acid

Short-answer questions

1 *(a)* **Name an element in:**
   (i) the same group of the Periodic Table as chlorine; **(1 mark)**
   (ii) the same period of the Periodic Table as carbon. **(1 mark)**
  (b) **Write down or draw a diagram of the electronic structure of:**
   (i) an atom of carbon (atomic number = 6);
   (ii) an atom of chlorine (atomic number = 17). **(2 marks)**
  (c) **Draw a diagram to show the electron arrangement in a molecule of tetrachloromethane (CCl_4). Only the outer electron shells need to be shown in your diagram.** **(2 marks)**
(SEG)

2 and *3* Use the Periodic Table in the Data Book to help you answer these questions.

2 Which group of the Periodic Table contains elements which form ions with a single positive charge? **(1 mark)**

3 Name two gases which are present in the atmosphere and which are in the same *period* as lithium. (2 marks)

4 Complete the following word equation:

sodium hydroxide + hydrochloric acid → ...... + ...

(1 mark)

5 Complete the following symbol equation:

Fe(s) + S(s) → ....

(1 mark)

(NEA)

Structured questions

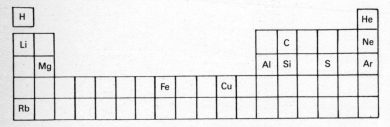

1 This question is about elements in the Periodic Table.

(a) Using only the symbols shown above, give the symbols for:

   (i)   an element which is in Group III of the Periodic Table;
   (ii) an element which forms an ion with a 2- charge;
   (iii) a non-metal used in making computer hardware;
   (iv) a metal used in making light alloys;
   (v)   an element that is used in illuminated signs;
   (vi) the element that reacts most violently with fluorine.

(6 marks)

(b) Place the symbol for each of the following elements in its correct place in the Periodic Table at the beginning of this question.

Element	Symbol	Atomic number
oxygen	O	8
calcium	Ca	20
bromine	Br	35

(3 marks)

(LEAG, syllabus B)

2 $1\,cm^3$ of 3.0M sodium hydroxide solution was added to $5\,cm^3$ of 1.0M iron(III) chloride solution in a test tube. After shaking to mix and allowing to stand for ten minutes, the height of the precipitate was measured. The experiment was repeated using different volumes of the 3.0M sodium hydroxide solution. The results are shown below:

Volume of 3.0M sodium hydroxide solution added/cm³	1	2	3	4	5	6	7
Height of the precipitate/mm	4	8	12	16	20	20	20

(a) On the grid below draw a graph of these results.

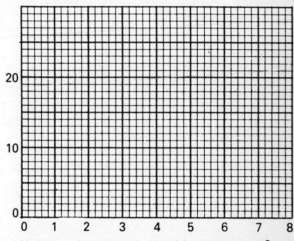

Height of precipitate /mm

Volume of sodium hydroxide solution./cm³

(2 marks)

(b) Explain why the height of the precipitate did not change from the 5th to the 7th cm³. (1 mark)

(c) Calculate the number of moles of sodium hydroxide in 5 cm³ of sodium hydroxide solution. (1 mark)

(d) The equation for the reaction is:

$$3NaOH(aq) + FeCl_3(aq) \rightarrow Fe(OH)_3(s) + 3NaCl(aq)$$

State the number of moles of iron(III) chloride required to react exactly with 5 cm³ of 3.0M sodium hydroxide solution. (1 mark)

(e) Show how the answer to *(d)* compares with the results of the experiment. (2 marks)

(f) Describe how you would attempt to obtain a pure dry sample of the precipitate formed in the experiment. (2 marks)

(LEAG, syllabus B)

3   Both egg shell and oyster shell contain calcium carbonate. This question is about an investigation into whether they both contain similar amounts of calcium carbonate.

    The calcium carbonate in the shells can be measured by reacting it with acid.

$$CaCO_3(s) + 2HCl(aq) \rightarrow CaCl_2(aq) + CO_2(g) + H_2O(l)$$

   (a) Why would a mixture of calcium carbonate and acid lose mass as it reacted?   (1 mark)
   (b) When acid is added to calcium carbonate a fine spray is often given off. Why would this cause an error in this investigation?
                                                                      (1 mark)
   (c) Draw a labelled diagram of the apparatus you would use to carry out the reaction between acid and egg shell or oyster shell.
                                                                      (4 marks)
   (d) List carefully the measurements you would make to carry out the investigation.   (4 marks)
   (e) How would you make sure that (i) the reaction between the acid and the shell has finished, and (ii) there is no more calcium carbonate left in the shell?   (2 marks)
   (f) How would your results tell you about the amounts of calcium carbonate in egg shells and oyster shell?   (3 marks)
                                                                      (SEG)

4   Many acidic substances are found in nature or in the home. These substances can be detected by the use of indicators.

   (a) (i) Name a suitable indicator to detect acids.
        (ii) What is observed when this indicator is placed in an acidic solution?   (2 marks)
   (b) The pH scale is used to indicate how acid or alkaline a substance is.

        (i) Give the name of a household substance that might have a pH of 5.
        (ii) A colourless liquid has a pH of 7. What does this indicate about the solution?   (2 marks)
   (c) The battery in a car contains fairly concentrated sulphuric acid. Explain why it is important not to spill any of the acid and how it could be neutralised using ordinary household substances.
                                                                      (3 marks)
                                                            (LEAG, syllabus A)

5   A portion of 0.1M hydrochloric acid was added to an excess of small pieces of magnesium ribbon. 120cm^3 of hydrogen were collected at room temperature and pressure. The equation for the reaction is:

$$Mg(s) + 2HCl(aq) \rightarrow MgCl_2(aq) + H_2(g)$$

(a) How many moles of hydrogen were collected? (Molar volume = 24dm^3 at room temperature and pressure.) (1 mark)

(b) What volume of 0.1M hydrochloric acid was used? (2 marks)

(c) What mass of magnesium is needed to produce this volume of hydrogen? (2 marks)

(d) On the grid below, sketch a graph to show the change in the volume of hydrogen collected during the course of the experiment. Label this graph A. (2 marks)

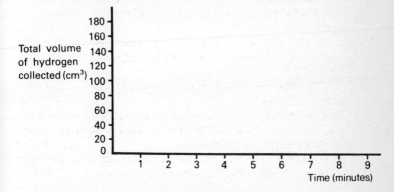

(e) On the same grid, sketch a graph showing the change in volume of hydrogen collected during the course of the experiment if the same volume of 0.1M hydrochloric acid had been added to an excess of *powdered* magnesium. Label this graph B. (2 marks)

(NEA)

Free-response questions

1 (a) State *three* differences in the properties of sodium chloride and tetrachloromethane (carbon tetrachloride). (3 marks)

(b) Explain in terms of the electronic structures of the compounds why they have these differences in properties. (6 marks)

(c) Use your knowledge of chemistry to explain the following facts as fully as you can.

(i) Aluminium wire carries electricity in power lines. (2 marks)

(ii) Graphite is used as a lubricant. (2 marks)

(NEA)

2 Describe how the position of elements in the Periodic Table is related to

(a) the chemical properties of the elements;

(b) the electron arrangements in the atoms of elements.

You should use your knowledge of the elements to give suitable examples to support the different points you wish to make.

Specimen answers are given on pages 95–100.

Chemical changes

Multiple-choice questions

1 Which of these substances decreases in mass when heated in air?

    A   carbon dioxide
    B   magnesium
    C   sodium chloride
    D   zinc carbonate

(SEG, Alt)

2 When dilute sulphuric acid is electrolysed using carbon electrodes, the gases produced at each electrode are:

	Cathode	*Anode*
A	CO_2	CO_2
B	O_2	H_2
C	CO_2	H_2
D	H_2	O_2
E	H_2	CO_2

(LEAG, syllabus B)

3 A chemical reaction occurs when:

    A   an electric current is passed through a copper wire
    B   salt solution is heated
    C   crude oil is distilled
    D   dilute hydrochloric acid is added to magnesium ribbon at room temperature
    E   ice melts to form water

(LEAG, syllabus A)

4 The rate of corrosion of a metal surface by an acid flowing over it in a chemical plant will be *decreased* by:

    A   increasing the concentration of the acid
    B   lowering the temperature of the acid
    C   adding air to the acid
    D   adding a catalyst
    E   giving the metal a rougher surface

5 Which one of the following describes what happens when a chemical is oxidised?

A   it loses heat
B   it moves up the reactivity series of metals
C   it has hydrogen added to it
D   it has oxygen taken away from it
E   it has oxygen added to it

Matching-pairs questions

Questions 1–5 relate to the following list of chemical changes:

A $C(s) + O_2(g) \rightarrow CO_2(g)\ \Delta H-ve$
B $Mg(s) + 2HCl(aq) \rightarrow MgCl_2(aq) + H_2(g)$
C $Cu^{2+}(aq) + 2e^- \rightarrow Cu(s)$
D $2H_2O(l) \rightarrow 2H_2(g) + O_2(g)\ \Delta H+ve$
E $HCl(aq) + NaOH(aq) \rightarrow NaCl(aq) + H_2O(l)$

Select from *A* to *E* the chemical change which:

1   is shown as being exothermic
2   is the overall chemical change when water is electrolysed
3   would be speeded up by using powdered metal as a reactant
4   involves oxidation of a non-metal
5   takes place at a cathode during electrolysis

Short-answer questions

1   The graph below shows the total volume of carbon dioxide produced in the reaction of chalk (calcium carbonate) with an excess of dilute hydrochloric acid over a period of time.

   (a) Use the graph to work out the volume of carbon dioxide pro-
       duced after 100 seconds.   (1 mark)
   (b) Draw on the graph the results you would expect to obtain if the
       same mass of calcium carbonate was reacted with:
       (i) more concentrated acid (label this 'A');
       (ii) less concentrated acid (label this 'B').   (2 marks)

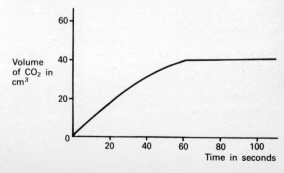

2 *(a)* Potassium bromide, KBr, is a salt which can be electrolysed when it is molten. During this process, what product would you expect to be formed:
   (i) at the positive electrode?
   (ii) at the negative electrode? (2 marks)
   (b) Why does solid potassium bromide NOT conduct electricity? (2 marks)
   (SEG)

3 $CuO + Mg \rightarrow MgO + Cu$ is an exothermic reaction.
   (a) What is meant by *exothermic*? (1 mark)
   (b) Name the reducing agent in this reaction. (1mark)
   (SEG)

4 Name an exothermic reaction which takes place in the human body.
5 Name an endothermic reaction which takes place in green plants

Structured questions

1 Ammonia is manufactured by making nitrogen and hydrogen react together at a moderate temperature and a high pressure in the presence of finely divided iron. The process is exothermic and the equation for the reaction is:

$$N_2(g) + 3H_2(g) \rightarrow 2NH_3(g)$$

The graphs below show the percentage yield of ammonia at different pressures and three different temperatures.

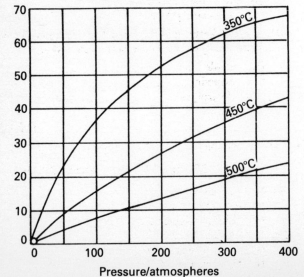

(a) Using the information contained in the graphs, describe how the amount of ammonia produced is affected by:

    (i)   changes of temperature;   **(1 mark)**

    (ii) changes of pressure.   **(1 mark)**

(b) What yield of ammonia would you expect to obtain if the reaction were carried out at 400°C and 300 atmospheres?

                                                       (1 mark)

(c) What is the purpose of the finely divided iron?   **(1 mark)**

(LEAG, syllabus B)

2 Liquid A is to be electrolysed.

(a) What type of power supply is suitable for this purpose? **(1 mark)**

(b) What piece of apparatus could be connected to X to show that liquid A is a conductor?   **(1 mark)**

(c) Give the name of the charged particles which conduct the electric current in:

    (i)   the connecting wires; ....

    (ii) the electrolyte ....   **(2 marks)**

(d) A metal kettle is to be coated with copper during electrolysis. State what you would use in the cell as the:

    (i)   anode ....

    (ii)   cathode ....

    (iii) electrolyte ....

                                                  (3 marks)

(LEAG, syllabus A)

3 For the reaction

$$SO_2(g) + 2H_2S(g) \rightarrow 3S(s) + 2H_2O(l)$$

(a) State which chemical is:

    (i)   oxidised to sulphur;   **(1 mark)**

    (ii) reduced to sulphur.   **(1 mark)**

(b) State which chemical is:

    (i)   the oxidising agent;   **(1 mark)**

    (ii) the reducing agent.   **(1 mark)**

(c) Explain why you said the chemical that you gave as the answer to *(a)*(i) is oxidised by the oxidising agent. (2 marks)

(d) Explain why you said the chemical that you gave as the answer to *(a)*(ii) is reduced by the reducing agent. (2 marks)

(e) Describe what you would see if the open end of a gas jar containing sulphur dioxide was placed against the open end of a gas jar containing hydrogen sulphide. (2 marks)

Free-response questions

1 Explain what we mean by the speed of a chemical reaction, and give an example of chemical changes which take place:

(a) very slowly;
(b) at a moderate speed;
(c) very quickly.

Give, with examples from your knowledge of chemistry, the different ways in which the speed of a chemical reaction can be changed, and explain how each of these methods has its effect.

2 Describe in your own words, with examples from your knowledge of chemistry, the different ways of defining:

(a) oxidation reactions, and
(b) reduction reactions.
(c) What relationship, if any, is there between oxidation–reduction and (i) electrolysis reactions; (ii) the reactivity series of metals

Specimen answers are given on pages 100–102.

Chemical resources

Multiple-choice questions

Questions *1–5* are concerned with fuels and their uses.
The pie chart below shows the amounts of different fuels consumed in Amazonia during 1975.

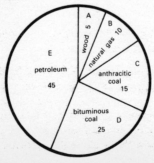

1 Which of the fuels A to E in the diagram is NOT a fossil fuel?

2 The element present in all these fuels is

    A   carbon
    B   chlorine
    C   helium
    D   neon
    E   sodium

3 In 1975, Amazonia's reserves of petroleum, bituminous coal and anthracitic coal were as follows:

	Available reserves in millions of tonnes
Petroleum	100
Bituminous coal	920
Anthracitic coal	140

If the amount of fuel consumed each year stays the same, the fuel(s) still available for use in the year 2000 will be

    A   all three
    B   both types of coal
    C   petroleum only
    D   bituminous coal only
    E   none of them

The table below gives the amount of heat energy that is released by 1 tonne of each fuel when it is burned in air.

	Energy release per tonne (arbitrary units)
Wood	4
Natural gas	41
Anthracitic coal	25
Bituminous coal	22
Petroleum	12

4 Natural gas burns more easily than the other fuels.
This is most probably because

    A   gases always burn better than solids and liquids
    B   the other fuels contain many substances which do not burn easily
    C   gases occupy a greater volume than do liquids and solids
    D   natural gas contains mostly methane
    E   gases mix better with the air, and therefore burn more quickly.

5 **The fuel which produced the most energy overall in 1975 was**

    A   **wood**
    B   **natural gas**
    C   **anthracitic coal**
    D   **bituminous coal**
    E   **petroleum**

(LEAG, syllabus B)

Matching-pairs questions

Questions *1–3* refer to the following chemical resources:

A   coal
B   natural gas
C   uranium
D   bauxite
E   gold

Select from *A–E* the chemical which

1 is the naturally occurring ore of the metal aluminium
2 is used in electric circuits
3 is used in generating nuclear power

Questions *4* and *5* refer to the following metals

A   iron
B   copper
C   aluminium
D   zinc
E   lead

Select from *A–E* the metal which

4 is used in car batteries
5 is used in water pipes and electrical circuits in modern houses

Short-answer questions

1 Identify the chemical resources described below:
    (a) A white metal used for making jewellery, and also widely used in industry as a chemical catalyst.   (1 mark)
    (b) A dark coloured liquid found under the ground in many parts of the world, which can be split up into a number of different fractions each of which has its own uses.   (1 mark)
    (c) A metal which is widely used for making objects which need to be physically strong, which can be extracted from its ore in a 'blast furnace', and which has to be protected from corrosion by moist air.   (1 mark)

2 *(a)* What is an alloy? (1 mark)

  (b) Name an alloy of iron. (1 mark)

  (c) Give two benefits that this alloy has over pure iron. (2 marks)

3

Compound	Formula	Mass of 1 mole/g	Percentage of elements by weight		
			N	P	K
Sodium nitrate	$NaNO_3$	85	16	–	–
Calcium phosphate	$Ca_3(PO_4)_2$	310	–	20	–
Ammonium phosphate	$(NH_4)_3PO_4$	149	28	21	–
Ammonium nitrate	NH_4NO_3	80	35	–	–
Potassium phosphate	K_3PO_4	212	–	15	18
Potassium chloride	KCl	74.5	–	–	52
Potassium nitrate	KNO_3	101	14	–	39

  (a) Which of these chemicals has the highest proportion by weight of nitrogen? (1 mark)

  (b) Explain why this would be the best nitrogen fertiliser to carry over long distances. (2 marks)

  (c) Which of the chemicals has the highest proportion by weight of potassium? (1 mark)

  (d) Why are 'NPK' values quoted on bags of fertiliser? (1 mark)

4 *(a)* Give two reasons why the element gold is used as a token of wealth. (2 marks)

  (b) Give two reasons why the element sodium is NOT used as a token of wealth. (2 marks)

5 *(a)* **Petrol is a mixture of liquids which are all hydrocarbons. What TWO elements are combined in petrol?** (1 mark)

  (b) **When a car has reached the end of its useful life it is normally crushed and the steel which it contains is recycled. Explain two reasons why it is important to do this rather than leaving a car to rust away on a scrap heap.** (4 marks)

  (LEAG, syllabus A, part question)

Structured questions

1 The table below includes the structural formulae of some monomers and the polymers that can be made from them.

Monomer	Polymer
 tetrafluoroethene	 polytetrafluoroethene
 chloroethene	polychloroethene
 propene	 polypropene

(a) Which one of the monomers is a hydrocarbon? (1 mark)

(b) The molecular formula of propene is C_3H_6. Write the molecular formula of chloroethene. (1 mark)

(c) Write in the table the structural formula of polychloroethene. (1 mark)

(d) What similarity in structure exists in the three monomers? (1 mark)

(e) What colour change would be observed if propene gas were bubbled through a solution of bromine?

The solution changes from . . . . to . . . . (2 marks)

(f) Addition polymers such as polyethene and polypropene are very difficult to dispose of.
  (i) Why are these polymers difficult to dispose of?

(ii) One possible method of disposal is burning. Name two possible products of combustion of polyethene and polypropene. (3 marks)

(g) The table below contains information about four materials in household refuse.

Material	Added to water
polymers	float on water
iron	sinks in water
aluminium	sinks in water
paper	floats on water

Paper, however, sinks in water when it is thoroughly wetted.

Assuming household refuse is a mixture only of polymers, paper, iron and aluminium, how could
(i) iron be removed from the refuse?
(ii) polymers be removed from the refuse? (3 marks)

(h) It is impossible at present to separate pure polyethene from household refuse. Usually the mixture of polymers is melted and made into cheaper blocks for lining walls.

(i) What properties of addition polymers are important in making and using these blocks?

Making the blocks . . . .

Using the blocks . . . .

(ii) What would be the economic advantage of being able to separate pure polyethene from household refuse? (3 marks)
(LEAG, syllabus B, part question)

2 Titanium is the seventh most abundant element in the earth's crust. One form in which it occurs is rutile, TiO_2.

In extracting titanium from its ore, rutile, it is first converted to titanium(IV) chloride, $TiCl_4$, and this is then reduced to the metal by heating it with sodium or magnesium in an atmosphere of argon.

(a) Write a balanced equation for the reaction of titanium(IV) chloride with sodium. (1 mark)

(b) Suggest a reason why it is necessary to carry out the reaction of titanium(IV) chloride with sodium in an atmosphere of argon.
(1 mark)

(c) Titanium is expensive in spite of the fact that it is relatively abundant in the earth's crust. Suggest a reason for this. (1 mark)

(d) Titanium is used in the structure of supersonic aircraft and space vehicles. Suggest TWO properties it might have that make it more suitable than other metals for this purpose. (2 marks)
(LEAG, syllabus A, part question)

Free-response questions

1 'Chemicals can act as energy stores.' Explain what you understand by this statement. How can chemicals become energy stores, and how can that energy be released? Give an example
   (a) from living matter;
   (b) from dead matter;
   of a chemical that is an energy store, and in each case explain how the energy was stored in the first place, and how it can be released.

2 Choose from your knowledge of chemistry a chemical substance that is useful, either directly or indirectly, in everyday life. Explain where the chemical is found, how it is obtained, and how it is used. State what you know about the amount that is used each year, the reserves of the chemical that we know about, and the length of time these reserves are likely to last.

Specimen answers are given on pages 102–105.

Chemical consequences

Multiple-choice questions

1 The amount of carbon dioxide in the air is *decreased* by
   A respiration
   B photosynthesis
   C the burning of fuel oil
   D the manufacture of calcium oxide from limestone
   E the extraction of iron
   (LEAG, syllabus A)

2 The most important reason for handling radioactive chemicals with care is that they
   A decay to form compounds of lead
   B emit particles which are electrically charged
   C emit particles which can make other substances radioactive
   D give off rays which can damage body tissues
   (SEG, Alt)

3 Which of the following is the chief reason that plastics are a pollution problem?
   A Plastics are organic compounds.
   B Plastics are resistant to bacterial action.
   C Plastics do not react readily with acid.
   D Plastics usually burn easily.
   (SEG, Alt)

4 Which of the following energy sources produces *least* problems for the environment of the atmosphere?

A   burning natural gas (methane, CH_4) in a gas stove

B   burning petrol in a car engine

C   producing electricity in a coal-powered power station

D   generation of electricity in a hydro-electric power station

5   Which of the following can follow from the use of too much fertiliser on the land?

    A   choking of ponds and streams with green algae on the surface ('eutrophication')

    B   an increase in the average temperature of the Earth's atmosphere ('the greenhouse effect')

    C   a decrease in the pH of rainwater falling in the area ('acid rain')

    D   a difficulty in forming a lather with soap using water from the land ('hard water')

Matching-pairs questions

Questions *1–5* refer to the following gases

A   carbon monoxide

B   nitrogen

C   water vapour

D   sulphur dioxide

E   carbon dioxide

1   Which gas is thought to be largely responsible for acid rain? D

2   Which gas passes through a car engine largely unchanged? C

3   Which gas is a poisonous part of car exhaust fumes? A

4   Which gas might be responsible for the 'greenhouse' effect in warming the earth, if there were too much of it in the air? E

5   Which gas is an element? B

Short-answer questions

Questions *1–4*: complete these sentences by filling the blank spaces.

1   **The incomplete combustion of petrol produces the poisonous gas called** ...... carbon monoxide

2   **The purest form of water which occurs naturally is** rainwater

3   **Drinking water which is good for the growth of healthy teeth and bones contains ions of the element** ... fluorine ...

4   **The name of a gas present in polluted air which can cause damage to buildings is** .. sulphur dioxide

(NEA, syllabus A)

5   Use of too much nitrogen fertiliser on the land can cause problems for pond life. The process which causes the pond life to die is called .... pollution ....

Structured questions

1 Most of the people in the world do not have enough to eat, so we must think of ways of growing more food. Sometimes chemicals are spread on the ground to provide food for plants.

   (a) What is the general name given to chemicals used by farmers to help plants grow? Fertilizer   (1 mark)

   (b) Ammonia is an important chemical used as a plant food.
       (i) Which Two elements are combined together to obtain ammonia? nitrogen, hydrogen
       (ii) From which raw materials are these elements obtained to make ammonia gas?
       .... and ....
                                                                (4 marks)

   (c) (i) Unfortunately these two elements combine together slowly so chemists use a catalyst. Name the catalyst used in making ammonia and explain its economic importance.
       (ii) Describe ONE other way in which chemists can speed up a reaction. Leahng   (3 marks)

   (d) Spreading chemicals on the land can have bad effects as well as good. Mention TWO bad things which might occur when chemicals are spread on the land. acid rain   (2 marks)
   killing plant in shec

   (e) (i) Give the chemical name of a polymer which can be used to make a bucket. Ethene
       (ii) Describe ONE advantage of the polymer material over steel for making a bucket. cheaper   (2 marks)

   (LEAG, syllabus A)

2 Petrol today contains small quantities of lead compounds to enable more petrol to be made from a given amount of petroleum. When the petrol burns in the car engine lead compounds escape into the atmosphere.

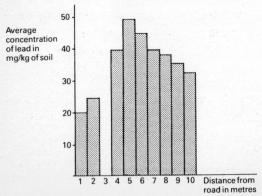

The bar chart shows the average concentrations of lead in soil samples at different distances from the edge of the road.

(a) What is the average concentration of lead in the soil 7 metres from the edge of the road? (2 marks)

(b) At a distance of 3 metres from the road the average concentration of lead is 33mg/kg of soil. Complete the bar chart by putting in this result. (1 mark)

(c) At what distance from the road is the average concentration of lead in soil greatest? (1 mark)

(d) Why is it wise to carry out experiments with several samples at each distance? (1 mark)

(e) Why is it unwise to grow vegetables in an allotment by the side of a busy road? (2 marks)

(f) Give one disadvantage of selling 'lead-free' petrol in place of 'leaded' petrol. (1 mark)

(LEAG, syllabus B)

Free-response questions

1 The Invergrog Reservoir Project

A.L. McHol and Co. are investigating the possibility of building a new whisky distillery on the Invergrog Industrial Estate. The proposed site is to the north-east of the town (see map on next page). Their big problem is where to get pure water from to make the whisky.

There are many streams flowing from the hills to the west of Invergrog. At first the company thought there were five possible places to build a small reservoir. These are shown and numbered on the map (1, 2, 3, 4 and 5). When samples of water taken from two of these locations were examined, they were found to contain too high a level of pollution. An analysis of water from a third possible site showed that it contained too many dissolved mineral salts.

Analysis of the mineral water from the third site (mg/dm³)

hydrogencarbonate	180.60	calcium	44.80
sulphate	10.00	magnesium	20.00
chloride	15.60	fluoride	0.06
nitrate	0.20	sodium	12.50

To help them choose between the two remaining sites the company carried out chemical tests to find the hardness of the water.

(a) Explain as fully as you can why the water at the two sites was polluted. (2 marks)

(b) What is the molarity of the mineral water with respect to sodium ions? (2 marks)

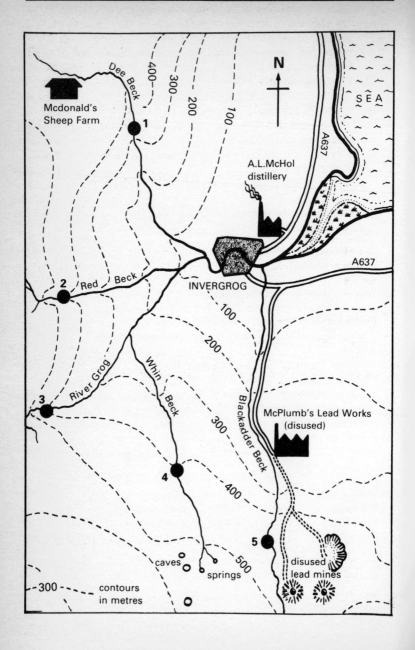

N

SEA

A637

Dee Beck

Mcdonald's
Sheep Farm

A.L.McHol
distillery

INVERGROG

A637

Red Beck

River Grog

Whin Beck

Blackadder Beck

McPlumb's Lead Works
(disused)

caves

springs

disused
lead mines

- 300 - contours
in metres

82

(c) Which of the ions present in this spring water are associated with hardness in water? (2 marks)

(d) Describe a simple method you could use to compare the hardness of the water from the two remaining sites. Your account should include the list of apparatus and chemicals you would use and details of how it is possible to make a fair comparison. (4 marks)

(e) If the distillery needed to use very soft water, it could be treated by using an ion-exchange column. Explain briefly how this process works. (2 marks)

(NEA, syllabus A)

2 The list below shows some processes which are used in industry.

cracking
fermentation
polymerisation

Using ONE example from industry in each case, describe briefly how each process may be used to manufacture a product useful in everyday life. *(LEAG, syllabus A)*

Specimen answers are given on pages 104–105.

Chemical techniques

Multiple-choice questions

1 The diagram represents the results when paper chromatography was used to identify the two herbicides present in a weedkiller.

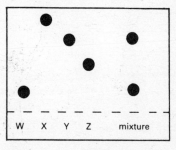

Which two substances are most likely to be present in the mixture?

A   X and Z
B   W and X
C   W and Y
D   Y and Z
E   W and Z

(LEAG, syllabus A)

2   A solid is likely to be pure if

   A   it is white
   B   it exists as crystals
   C   it does not react with other chemicals
   D   it melts at the same temperature, even after several re-
         crystallisations
   E   on electrolysis it always gives the same products

(LEAG, syllabus B)

3   When excess magnesium is added to hydrochloric acid the following
   reaction occurs:

$$Mg(s) + 2HCl(aq) \longrightarrow MgCl_2(aq) + H_2(g)$$

   The first process needed after the reaction to obtain pure crystals of
   magnesium chloride is

   A   distillation
   B   evaporation
   C   filtration
   D   neutralisation

(SEG, Alt)

4   The following table shows the solubility of a number of substances.

Substance	Solubility in water
barium sulphate	insoluble
calcium sulphate	slightly soluble
lead(II) nitrate	soluble
lead(II) oxide	insoluble
lead(II) sulphate	insoluble
sodium sulphate	soluble

   Which of the following pairs of substances would be most suitable
   for preparing lead sulphate for use as a white pigment in paint?

   A   lead(II) oxide and sodium sulphate
   B   lead(II) nitrate and sodium sulphate
   C   lead(II) oxide and barium sulphate
   D   lead(II) nitrate and barium sulphate
   E   lead(II) nitrate and calcium sulphate

(LEAG, syllabus A)

5   A solid suitable for purification by crystallisation from water is likely
   to
   A   dissolve in cold water but not in hot water
   B   be insoluble in hot and cold water

C   be very soluble in cold water
D   react with water to form a precipitate
E   be more soluble in hot water than in cold water

(LEAG, syllabus A)

Matching-pairs questions

Questions *1–5* relate to the following practical methods:

A   chromatography
B   crystallisation
C   distillation
D   electrolysis
E   filtration

Choose from *A* to *E* the method which would be used to

1   isolate nitrogen from liquid air
2   separate coloured substances in a sample of coloured soft drink
3   separate petrol from crude oil
4   separate a drug which has been precipitated from a solution

(LEAG, syllabus A)

5   obtain crystals of potassium nitrate from its aqueous solution

(LEAG, syllabus B)

Short-answer questions

1   What is the volume of liquid in this measuring cylinder?

.... cm^3

(NEA, syllabus A)

2   This is used to test for the gas called

....

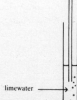

(NEA, syllabus A)

3 This bar chart shows the average amount of sulphur dioxide in town air. In 1981, the average was 120 micrograms/metre^3. Add this information to the chart.

(NEA, syllabus A)

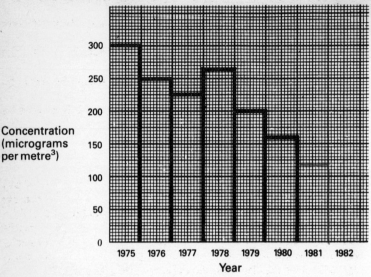

4 Complete the table below, which describes the preparation of some salts.

REACTANTS			PRODUCTS		
maganesium oxide	+	→	magnesium sulphate	+	
	+	→	zinc chloride	+	hydrogen
	+ sodium sulphate	→	lead sulphate	+	

(6 marks)
(SEG)

5 Complete the diagram of the apparatus used to electrolyse copper sulphate solution.

(NEA, syllabus A)

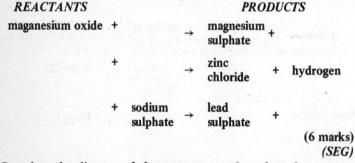

Structured questions

1 Read the following instructions about how to make zinc sulphate crystals. It is done by reacting white zinc oxide with a suitable acid.

(i) Place 25 cm^3 of the acid in a beaker and raise its temperature to about $80\,^\circ\text{C}$.

(ii) Remove the beaker from the heat, then add the oxide one spatula at a time, stirring well.

(iii) When no more solid will react, separate the oxide from the solution.

(iv) Evaporate away the water in the solution, until it is ready to crystallise.

(v) Allow the solution to cool and crystallise.

Now answer questions *(a)* to *(g)* below.

(a) What acid would you use? (1 mark)

(b) Why is the acid warmed in (i)? (1 mark)

(c) How would you know that no more oxide would react in (iii)? (1 mark)

(d) Why will no more oxide react in (iii)? (1 mark)

(e) How would you do the separation in (iii)? (1 mark)

(f) Why does the clear solution in (v) crystallise as it cools? (1 mark)

(g) Why is all the water not boiled away in (iv)? (1 mark)

(NEA, syllabus B)

2 Oxygen gas can be prepared conveniently in the laboratory using the apparatus below. The manganese dioxide is a *catalyst*: a substance which speeds up the reaction but is not used up at all.

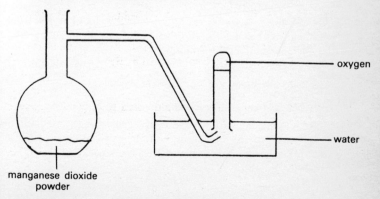

(a) Complete the diagram by drawing the apparatus you would use to add the hydrogen peroxide solution in controlled amounts.

87

(b) Why is the first test tube of gas not used?

(c) (i) Is oxygen very soluble in water?

     (ii) What evidence have you, from this experiment, to support your answer?

(d) How can you prove the gas collected was oxygen?

     (i) What would you do?

     (ii) What would you see?

(e) How could a dry sample of manganese dioxide be obtained from the flask after the reaction? (two steps).

(NEA, syllabus B)

Free-response questions

1 The labels have become unreadable on three bottles which were known to contain

    ammonium chloride;   calcium carbonate;   iron(II) sulphate

What *chemical* tests would you carry out to enable you to relabel the bottles correctly? Your answer must include at least *one positive*, *chemical* test for each substance that would NOT be given by any of the others.

(LEAG, syllabus A)

2 Aspirin is an acid which may be represented by the formula H^+A^-, where A^- is a complicated organic ion. Aspirin itself is not very soluble but its sodium salt, known as 'soluble aspirin', dissolves easily in cold water. Addition of dilute hydrochloric acid to a solution of soluble aspirin causes aspirin to appear as a precipitate.

(a) Describe carefully how you would prepare a sample of pure dry aspirin from a solution of soluble aspirin, explaining why your method is appropriate.

(b) Theoretically you would expect to obtain 178g of aspirin from 200g of soluble aspirin. Explain carefully why you would actually get less than this amount.

(LEAG, syllabus A)

Specimen answers are given on pages 105–107.

Questions drawn from many areas

Many questions on examination papers, especially longer, structured questions and free-response questions, contain material drawn from a number of different areas of chemistry. Here are a few examples.

Structured questions

1 This question is about the formation of alcohol (ethanol) from sugars and its possible use as an alternative to petrol as a fuel for car engines.

One source of sugars is sugar cane which is crushed and the juices mixed with yeast. The mixture is allowed to stand for two or three days at around $30^\circ C$.

The liquid product is then fractionally distilled, most of the ethanol being in these fractions.

(a) Name *one* other crop which is a useful source of sugars.

(1 mark)

(b) The equation for the reaction which changes the sugar glucose into ethanol in the presence of yeast is given below:

$$C_6H_{12}O_6 \text{ (aq)} \rightarrow 2C_2H_5OH \text{ (aq)} + 2CO_2 \text{ (g)}$$

(i)   What does the symbol (aq) indicate about the glucose?

(1 mark)

(ii) What is the purpose of the yeast in the reaction?   (1 mark)

(iii) Why is this reaction *not* speeded up if the mixture is boiled?   (1 mark)

(iv) Give the name of the process which converts glucose into ethanol in this way.   (1 mark)

(v)   Why is the same reaction important in bread-making?

(1 mark)

(c) One of the advantages of ethanol over petrol is that, unlike petrol, ethanol is a *renewable energy source*. Explain the meaning of the term *renewable energy source*.   (1 mark)

(d) What other possible advantages might ethanol have over petrol as a fuel for car engines?   (2 marks)

(e) Methylated spirits is a mixture of ethanol (about 90%) and methanol (about 10%) together with a small quantity of purple dye.

Explain why the ethanol is treated in this way before being sold as 'meths'.   (3 marks)

(SEG, Alternative)

2 The diagram below shows the electrolysis of concentrated sodium chloride solution.

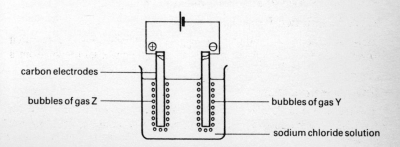

carbon electrodes

bubbles of gas Z

bubbles of gas Y

sodium chloride solution

(a) Name the gases Y and Z. (2 marks)

(b) If a few drops of universal indicator are added to the solution before electrolysis starts, the indicator is green. As electrolysis happens, the indicator gradually turns blue.

    (i) What is the pH of the solution when the indicator is green? (1 mark)

    (ii) Explain why the electrolysis causes the indicator to go blue. (3 marks)

    (iii) Name a compound produced on an industrial scale by electrolysis of sodium chloride solution. (1 mark)

(c) In the electrolysis of copper(II) chloride solution the electron transfer at the negative electrode is shown by the following equation:

$$Cu^{2+}(aq) + 2e^- \rightarrow Cu(s)$$

    (i) What does (aq) stand for? (1 mark)

    (ii) What would you expect to *see* at the positive electrode during this electrolysis? (2 marks)

(d) The table gives information about three substances A, B and C when they are solid and when they are molten.

	SOLID SUBSTANCE		MOLTEN SUBSTANCE		
Substance	Appearance of solid	Does the solid conduct electricity?	Does the melt conduct electricity?	Product at + electrode	Product at − electrode
A	white solid	no	yes	bromine	lead metal
B	yellow solid	no	no	(does not conduct)	
C	grey solid	yes	yes	none	none

    (i) Suggest possible identities for substances A and B. (2 marks)

    (ii) What type of bonding does solid B have? (1 mark)

    (iii) What type of bonding does solid C have? (1 mark)

    (iv) When the melted substance A conducts electricity what particles are carrying the current? (1 mark)

(e) (i) Predict the products of electrolysis of an aqueous solution of aluminium sulphate using inert electrodes. Explain how you arrive at your answer. (4 marks)

    (ii) Why is cryolite added to aluminium oxide during the electrolytic manufacture of aluminium? (1 mark)

(SEG)

3 The table below gives information about four elements, V, W, X and Y, which are in the same group in the Periodic Table.

Element	Atomic Number	Melting point/°C	Boiling point/°C
V	9	−220	−188
W	17	−101	−33
X	35	−7	58
Y	53	114	183

(a) Use the melting and boiling points to give the letters of all the elements in the table which, at atmospheric pressure and at room temperature, are
   (i)   solids;
   (ii) liquids;
   (iii) gases. (3 marks)

(b) Describe what happens to the particles of a solid when it melts to form a liquid. (3 marks)

(c) The next element in this group after Y is Z.
   (i) Would you expect Z to exist under room conditions as a solid, liquid or gas? State your reasons.
   (ii) How many electrons will there be in the outer shell of a Z atom?
   (iii) Using the symbol Z, write down the formula of the ion of Z. (4 marks)

(LEAG, syllabus A, part question)

(d) In a reaction, 0.17g of W were found to react with 0.4g of a metal (M) according to the equation

$$2M + W_2 \rightarrow 2MW$$

If the relative atomic mass of W is 35.5, what is the relative atomic mass of the metal M?

Free-response question

An experiment was carried out to find the formula of a metal iodide by reacting a known mass of metal (M) with excess iodine. The excess iodine was removed by extracting with ethanol and the product completely dried.

(a) From the results below calculate the formula of the iodide of the metal (Relative atomic masses: M = 65, I = 127).

Mass of empty tube   = 4.75g
Mass of tube and metal   = 5.55g
Mass of tube and metal iodide   = 8.67g

(b) Discuss the reactivity series of the halogens in terms of the displacement of their ions from aqueous solution.

(NEA, syllabus A)

Specimen answers are given on pages 107–109.

SECTION 6
Specimen answers

Answers are given in the same order in which the corresponding questions appeared in Section 5.

Chemical substances (see page 53)

Multiple-choice questions

1 B *2* C *3* D *4* E *5* E

Matching-pairs questions

1 E *2* E *3* E *4* D *5* E

Short-answer questions

1 *(a)* photosynthesis
  (b) water
  (c) e.g. coal formed from plants; oil formed from animals.

2 *(a)* e.g. add dilute sulphuric acid; copper(II) oxide forms blue solution, carbon does not react.
  (b) e.g. magnesium burns with brilliant light in air, iron does not burn.

3 chlorine

4 proteins

5 oxygen

Structured questions

1 *(a)* (i) oxygen (ii) copper(II) oxide (iii) pink/brown to black
    (iv) nitrogen
  (b) (i) Any suitable example, e.g. burning.
       Give chemical description or equation.
    (ii) $19\,cm^3$–$21\,cm^3$ (inclusive) accepted.
    (iii) Immerse glowing splint in the gas. Splint relights.

2 *(a)* any two sources from those given
  (b) zinc sulphide

(c) oxygen is added

(d) (i) reversible reaction   (ii) air

(e) (i) speeds up production of sulphuric acid (or, more acid can be produced under the given conditions).

(ii) sulphur dioxide is purified

(f) (i) waste of valuable raw material (1 mark)

(ii) two suitable points, e.g. forms an acid, acid rain, effect on buildings, trees etc. (3 marks)

(g) sulphur trioxide + water → sulphuric acid

$$SO_3 + H_2O \rightarrow H_2SO_4$$

3 (a) (i) Compound which contains carbon (1 mark) and hydrogen, often in conjunction with other elements (1 mark)

(ii) Substance which burns in a controlled way in air to produce energy (1 mark)

(iii) Substance in which all the atoms are alike (1 mark) and which cannot be decomposed to produce other elements (1 mark)

(b) (i) hydrogen, oxygen (1 mark each)

(ii) sulphur dioxide (2 marks) ('oxide' gains 1 mark)

(c) as a fertiliser

(d) calcium sulphate

(e) (i) gold, silver, platinum, mercury (any one of these)

(ii) too reactive

(f) Any suitable use, e.g. electrical wiring (1 mark)

Explanation: good conductor (1 mark)

4 (a) (i) calcium chloride   (ii) water

(b) (i) heavier than air   (ii) does not allow combustion   (iii) fire extinguisher

(c) (i) carbon   (ii) magnesium oxide

(iii) magnesium + carbon dioxide → magnesium oxide + carbon

5 (a) first two boxes under 'phosphorus'

(b) (i) silicon   (ii) high melting point

(c) phosphorus, sulphur, chlorine

(d) sodium, magnesium (also aluminium)

(e) (i) molecular   (ii) 170

(iii) $SiCl_4(l) + 2H_2O(l) \rightarrow SiO_2(s) + 4HCl(aq)$

(You know $SiCl_4$ is not a solid from its melting point)

Free-response questions

1 This question can be answered at a variety of levels. To get maximum marks, it would be necessary to discuss all the different aspects mentioned in the question (there were four of them). Chemical information which you would need to use in such an answer includes the following:

the reactions which take place;
the catalyst used and its cost, ease of poisoning;
the energy changes involved;
the nature of the chemicals involved and their effect on the environment if allowed to escape;
the form in which the acid is kept - its chemical and physical nature;
the chemicals and materials made from sulphuric acid.

Try to show what you know about the manufacture and importance of sulphuric acid, and use your knowledge and understanding of the chemistry involved.

2 As above, you need to mention all aspects asked for in the question if you are to get full marks. You would need to use the following information:

the physical and chemical properties of iron, illustrated by uses;
the nature of its ore and where this is found;
the chemical reactions involved in the extraction of iron;
the different alloys which can be made from iron, and their uses.

Try to show what you know about iron as a chemical, and about its uses, and use you knowledge and understanding of the chemistry involved.

Chemical models (see pages 61-8)

Multiple-choice questions

1 B *2* D *3* C *4* A *5* D

Matching-pairs questions

1 A (group I or group II) *2* E (inert gas) *3* B (transition metals)
4 A (must be group II, because two electrons in outermost shell)
5 D (element is sulphur, a non-metal)

Short-answer questions

1 *(a)* (i) fluorine (or bromine, iodine, astatine)
         (ii) lithium (or beryllium, boron, nitrogen, oxygen, fluorine, neon)

(b) (i) 2,4   (ii) 2, 8, 7

or

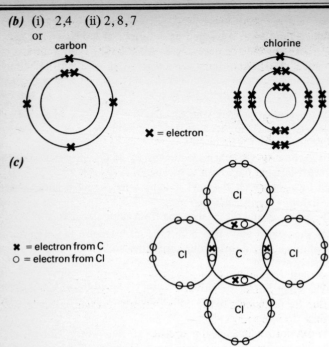

carbon   chlorine

✗ = electron

(c)

✗ = electron from C
○ = electron from Cl

Cl

Cl   C   Cl

Cl

2 group I (alkali metals)
3 nitrogen, oxygen
4 sodium chloride + water
5 $FeS_2(s)$

Structured questions

1 **(a)** (i) Al (ii) S (iii) Si (iv) Al (v) Ne (vi) Rb
   (b) oxygen – two boxes to the right of C
       calcium – underneath Mg
       bromine – between S and Ar, but in row below

2 **(a)**

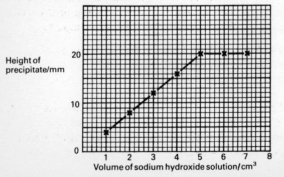

Height of
precipitate/mm

Volume of sodium hydroxide solution/cm³

(b) All Fe^{3+} had been precipitated or used up; or, no further reaction took place.

(c) $1000 cm^3$ 3.0M NaOH contains 3 moles NaOH

∴ $5 cm^3$ 3.0M NaOH contains $\dfrac{5 \times 3}{1000}$ moles

$$= 0.015 \text{ moles NaOH}$$

(d) 3 moles NaOH require 1 mole $FeCl_3$

∴ 0.015 moles NaOH require 0.005 moles $FeCl_3$

(e) From the experiment

$5 cm^3$ 1.0M $FeCl_3$ react with $5 cm^3$ 3.0M NaOH

∴ 1 mole $FeCl_3$ reacts with 3 moles NaOH

(f) Filter, or centrifuge and decant

Wash with water

Dry

(All three steps needed for full marks.)

3 *(a)* Because carbon dioxide gas is formed and this is lost.

(b) The spray would carry away some of the reactant chemicals.

(c) Burette containing acid, above suitable reaction vessel (conical flask, to trap spray).

(d) Weigh out x g of powdered egg shell.

Weigh out y g of powdered oyster shell.

Titrate each with dilute hydrochloric acid of known concentration, taking reading on burette before and after titration.

(e) (i) Could carry on until no more 'fizz', or use a suitable indicator, or place flask on top-pan balance and check no weight loss due to carbon dioxide being given off (any one of these responses).

(ii) Check solution left at end still contains acid.

(f) A known mass of egg shell has reacted with a known volume of dilute hydrochloric acid. So the number of moles, and therefore the mass of calcium carbonate contained, can be calculated. Can then work out percentage by mass of egg shell which is calcium carbonate. Repeat for oyster shell and compare.

4 *(a)* (i) litmus, universal indicator etc.

(ii) for litmus – goes red, etc.

(b) (i) coffee (or lemonade)

(ii) it is neutral.

(c) The acid is corrosive by reaction with e.g. iron, and burns skin by dehydration.

Suitable substance for neutralisation would be household bleach.

Alkali neutralises acid.

5 (a) 1 mole occupies $24\,000\,cm^3$

$\therefore$ $120cm^3$ contains $\dfrac{120}{24000}$ moles

$$= 0.005 \text{ moles.}$$

(b) 2 moles HCl give 1 mole H_2

$\therefore$ 0.01 moles HCl give 0.005 moles H_2

$1000\,cm^3$ 1.0M HCl contains 1 mole

$\therefore$ $1000\,cm^3$ 0.1M HCl contains 0.1 mole

$\therefore$ $100\,cm^3$ 0.1M HCl contains 0.01 mole

(c) 1 mole Mg gives 1 mole H_2

$\therefore$ 0.005 moles Mg gives 0.005 moles H_2

1 mole Mg weighs 24g

0.005 moles Mg weighs 24×0.005 g

$$= 0.12\,g$$

(d) and (e)

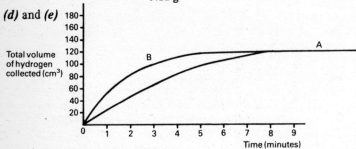

(Powdered magnesium reacts more quickly than solid magnesium, but the same amount of reaction takes place, so the final amount of hydrogen obtained is the same.)

Free-response questions

1 (a) These could be any of the properties which would be different for an ionic compound (sodium chloride) and a molecular compound (tetrachloromethane). So you could mention any three of:

> melting point and boiling point (higher for ionic compound);
> electrical conductivity of molten compound (ionic compound conducts, molecular compound does not);
> speed of reactivity (high for ionic compound, low for molecular);
> solubility in water (high for ionic compound, low for molecular);

solubility in organic solvent (high for molecular compound, low for ionic).

(b) First, you would need to describe what the electronic structures are – oppositely charged ions as a result of electron transfer for sodium chloride, and molecules as a result of electron sharing for tetrachloromethane. For each of the three properties mentioned above, you should then explain the difference in terms of the electronic structures of the two compounds.

> *Melting point and boiling point* – in terms of the forces of attraction between particles. High for ionic compounds, low for molecular.
>
> *Electrical conductivity* – in terms of the ability of ions to 'carry' an electric current by movement to and discharge at oppositely charged electrode. Inability of molecules to do this.
>
> *Speed of reactivity* – need for bonds to be broken and reformed in molecular compound causes reactions to be slower than for ionic compounds where ions simply 'rearrange' during reactions.
>
> *Solubility* – need for 'polar' solvent such as water in the case of ionic compounds, and attraction between opposite charges causing dissolving. Need for non-polar molecules to have non-polar solvent such as typical organic solvent.

(c) (i) You are being asked to explain how metals conduct electricity. You will need to explain the structure of metals, and how electrons form a 'cloud' around close-packed metal atoms. Thus an electron entering at one end of a piece of metal results in an electron leaving at the other (electrical conductivity). A diagram would make explanation easier.

(ii) Here, you must describe the 'layer' structure of graphite (again, use a diagram to save words). Explain the weak forces between the layers as compared to the strong forces within layers. Thus the layers can 'slip', and the substance acts as a lubricant.

2 *(a)* First of all, you must outline the shape of the Periodic Table – how many groups and how many periods. Draw a diagram. Then go on to state that elements with similar properties are in the same group (column). Give an example (e.g. Group 1), with some examples of similar properties (e.g. reaction with water).

Next, you should explain the gradual change in properties from one group in the table to the next – right across the table. Choose a period (row), and use it to show how strong metallic behaviour gives way to weak metallic behaviour, weak non-metallic behaviour, and finally strong non-metallic behaviour.

Mention the Group 0 elements (inert gases) and the transition metals.

(b) Start by describing the maximum number of electrons allowed in the first three shells of atoms. Then explain how successive electrons go into the next available space of lowest energy – resulting in an orderly build up of the electron arrangements for the different elements.

Group 0 is a good place to start relating electron arrangements to properties. Show that filled electron shells lead to chemical inertness.

Then choose elements from Group 1 and Group 7 to show strong metallic behaviour (electron donation) and strong non-metallic behaviour (electron acceptance and sharing). Show that metals and non-metals react together to form ionic compounds, and that non-metals react with other non-metals to form molecular compounds.

Explain why a metal such as aluminium is less strongly metallic than e.g. sodium (more electrons to lose) and why e.g. silicon is less strongly non-metallic than e.g. chlorine (more electrons to gain/share).

Chemical changes (see pages 68–72)

Multiple-choice questions

1 D   *2* D   *3* D   *4* B   *5* E

Matching-pairs questions

1 A   *2* D   *3* B   *4* A   *5* C

Short-answer questions

1 (a)   40 cm^3

    (b)

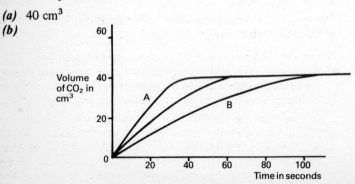

2 *(a)* (i) bromine   (ii) potassium
   (b) Ions are not free to move in the solid.

3 *(a)* Heat is given out to the surroundings.

   (b) magnesium (it takes oxygen away from copper(II) oxide)

4 respiration

5 photosynthesis

Structured questions

1 *(a)* (i) (At constant pressure) reducing temperature gives a higher yield.
       (ii) (At constant temperature) raising pressure gives a higher yield.
   (b) any answer in the range 45% to 55%
   (c) catalyst (or, large surface area)

2 *(a)* one supplying a direct current
   (b) ammeter or lamp
   (c) (i) electrons   (ii) ions
   (d) (i) piece of copper   (ii) the kettle   (iii) copper(II) sulphate solution

3 *(a)* (i) hydrogen sulphide (H_2S)   (ii) sulphur dioxide (SO_2)
   (b) (i) sulphur dioxide (SO_2)   (ii) hydrogen sulphide (H_2S)
   (c) Hydrogen is removed.
   (d) Oxygen is removed.
   (e) You would see a yellow mist, which results in a coating of yellow solid on the inside of both gas jars.

Free-response questions

1 The speed of a chemical reaction is the rate at which products form, or the rate at which reactants are used up.

   (a) A very slow reaction would be rusting (give equation).
   (b) A reaction of moderate speed would be the reaction between magnesium ribbon and dilute hydrochloric acid (give equation).
   (c) An explosion is a very rapid reaction, e.g. $2H_2 + O_2 \rightarrow 2H_2O$.

   You should list the different factors which can alter the speed of a chemical reaction (temperature, concentration, pressure, presence of catalyst, state of division of a solid reactant, etc.). Explain how the rate of a chemical reaction depends on the number of collisions between particles in a given time, and the energy of those collisions.

Explain how the different factors mentioned above have their effect through the way they change the number of collisions, the energy of collisions or the effective activation energy of the reaction.

2 *(a)* Define oxidation in terms of oxygen gain, hydrogen loss and electron loss.

(b) Define reduction in terms of hydrogen gain, oxygen loss and electron gain.

For each of the six definitions, give an example, with equation. Explain how the sample shows the particular process, in each case.

(c) (i) Explain how the electrode equations might be considered: reduction (at cathode), e.g. $Cu^{2+} + 2e^- \rightarrow Cu$

and oxidation (at anode), e.g. $Cu \rightarrow Cu^{2+} + 2e^-$

(ii) Explain how reactions between metal and metal cation can be considered redox reactions, e.g. $Mg + Cu^{2+} \rightarrow Mg^{2+} + Cu$ (Mg oxidized, Cu^{2+} reduced).

So reactivity series of metals is really a list of relative strength as a reducing agent of the metal.

Chemical resources (see pages 72–8)

Multiple-choice questions

1 A   *2* A   *3* D   *4* E   *5* D

Matching-pairs questions

1 D   *2* E   *3* C   *4* E   *5* B

Short-answer questions

1 *(a)* platinum   *(b)* petroleum   *(c)* iron

2 *(a)* a substance made by mixing a pure metal with a small amount of another element
   (b) steel
   (c) Stronger. Can be made 'stainless'.

3 *(a)* ammonium nitrate
   (b) For the same energy, and therefore for the same cost, more nitrogen could be moved.
   (c) potassium chloride
   (d) So that the person buying the fertiliser knows how much each of the three elements is in a given weight of fertiliser. Some crops and some soils need one element, some another.

4 (a) Rare. Does not tarnish.

   (b) Too reactive (never found naturally as a solid). Not hard enough to be made into coins.

5 (a) carbon, hydrogen

   (b) Any two of the following pairs of reasons and explanations:

       Cars on scrap heap are unsightly (they only corrode slowly).

       To conserve steel (iron is in limited supply).

       It is cheaper to extract iron from car bodies than from ore (it is already fairly pure).

Structured questions

1 (a) propene

   (b) C_2H_3Cl

   (c)

$$\left[\begin{array}{cc} H & Cl \\ | & | \\ -C & -C- \\ | & | \\ H & H \end{array} \right]_n$$

   (d) double bond

   (e) from red to colourless

   (f) (i) do not rot away

       (ii) carbon, carbon monoxide, carbon dioxide, water

   (g) (i) magnet

       (ii) Add to water. Scoop polymers from top after paper sinks.

   (h) (i) easily melted; good insulation

       (ii) recycling of resources; less cost.

2 (a) $TiCl_4 + 4Na \rightarrow Ti + 4NaCl$

   (b) to prevent oxidation of Ti

   (c) cost of extraction is high

   (d) strong, light etc.

Free-response questions

1 You should describe the way in which energy can be stored during a chemical reaction which takes in energy from the surroundings, because of the relative strengths of the chemical bonds in all the reactants compared with the strengths of the chemical bonds in all the products. This process is reversed when one of the products is used as a fuel or energy source, in an exothermic reaction.

   You could describe the production of sugar by photosynthesis in a green plant, and the use of sugar to provide energy during respiration. You should give word equations or balanced symbol equations for the reactions involved, and show which reaction is exothermic and which is endothermic.

A similar example from dead matter would be methane (natural gas) produced by the decay of dead animal matter, which can then be used as a fuel in combustion. Again, give equations for any reactions which you mention.

2 Choose the chemical substance that you can give the fullest answer for. It might be iron, or calcium carbonate, or petroleum, or gold, or some other. Make sure, whichever chemical you choose, that you can use this question to show what you know and to show your understanding of the chemical principles involved. Where you describe any extraction process, explain the type of reaction (electrolysis or reduction of oxide? Why?) and give equations. Give the chemistry that you know about when it comes to uses of the chemical. Mention the economic importance of the chemical, and explain what consequences there might be if it is one of those chemical resources which may not have a long future.

Chemical consequences (see pages 78–83)

Multiple-choice questions

1 B   *2* D   *3* B   *4* D   *5* A

Matching-pairs questions

1 D   *2* B   *3* A   *4* E   *5* B

Short-answer questions

1 carbon monoxide
2 rain water
3 calcium
4 sulphur dioxide
5 eutrophication

Structured questions

1 *(a)* fertilisers
   (b) (i) nitrogen, hydrogen   (ii) air and the cracking of petroleum
   (c) (i) Iron. It increases the rate of production of ammonia and so greater profitability.
      (ii) heating (or some other suitable answer)
   (d) (i) Leaching of chemicals into rivers etc.
      (ii) Herbicides and pesticides can enter food chains. (Or some other suitable answer.)
   (e) (i) polyethene or polypropylene
      (ii) tougher, or resistant to rusting, or resistant to chemicals. (Or some other suitable answer.)

2 *(a)* 40mg/kg of soil
   (b) one mark for a correct recording on the chart
   (c) 5m
   (d) A single sample may not be a typical sample. (Or some other similar answer.)
   (e) Lead is taken in by plants. Lead is poisonous.
   (f) Unleaded petrol is more expensive. Some cars cannot use it. (Or some other suitable reason.)

Free-response questions

1 (a) The two polluted sites must have been 1 and 5. At 1, sheep droppings etc. would find their way into the water, polluting it with bacteria and other organisms. At 5, lead ions washed down from lead ore in the mines would pollute the water.

(b) Water contains 12.5mg of sodium per dm^3
   $= 0.0125g$ of sodium per dm^3.

   A solution molar in Na^+ ions would contain 23g of sodium per dm^3.
   $\therefore$ Molarity is $\dfrac{0.0125M}{23} = 5.4 \times 10^{-4}M$

(c) calcium ions

(d) Hardness depends on concentration of calcium ions. So, for example, take known volume of solution, react with excess sodium carbonate solution, filter off precipitate, dry and weigh.

(e) Explain principle of exchange of harmless ions such as Na^+ or H^+ on resin for unwanted ions (Ca^{2+}).

2 In each case, you should give the raw materials used, describe the process (with an equation if possible) and explain why the process is important. Use the question to show what you know about industrial processes which depend on these processes, and what you understand of the chemical principle and economic importance which are involved.

Chemical techniques (see pages 83–8)

Multiple-choice questions

1 C   *2* D   *3* C   *4* B   *5* E

Matching-pairs questions

1 C   *2* A   *3* C   *4* E   *5* B

Short-answer questions

1 24ml (cm^3) *2* carbon dioxide   *3* –
4 (i)   dilute sulphuric acid; water

(ii) zinc; dilute hydrochloric acid
(iii) lead nitrate; sodium nitrate

Structured questions

1 (a) dilute sulphuric acid
   (b) To make it react more quickly (also to help with crystallisation).
   (c) Some solid would remain.
   (d) All the acid has been used up.
   (e) By filtration
   (f) Because zinc sulphate is more soluble in hot water than in cold water.
   (g) Would not allow good crystals to form.

2 (a) tap funnel
   (b) contains air from inside the apparatus
   (c) (i) no   (ii) oxygen is collected 'over water'.
   (d) (i) Place glowing splint in gas.   (ii) Splint would be relighted.
   (e) Filter. Dry in air.

Free-response questions

1 There is a variety of possible answers to this question. You should use it to show what you know about the chemical tests to identify the substances involved, and what you understand about the chemical principles which you are using.

For example, you could

(1) Heat each with dilute sodium hydroxide solution, and test the gas given off. Only ammonium chloride would result in ammonia being formed: $NH_4Cl(s) + NaOH(aq) \rightarrow NaCl(aq) + NH_3(g) + H_2O(l)$.
Ammonia gas turns moist litmus paper from red to blue.
Iron(II) sulphate would give a blue/green jelly-like precipitate of iron(II) hydroxide: $Fe^{2+}(aq) + 2OH^-(aq) \rightarrow Fe(OH)_2(s)$.

(2) Add dilute hydrochloric acid to each. Only calcium carbonate would result in carbon dioxide being formed:
$CaCO_3(s) + 2HCl(aq) \rightarrow CaCl_2(aq) + CO_2(g) + H_2O(l)$
Carbon dioxide turns limewater milky.

2 (a) You are being asked to show what you know and understand about the process of obtaining a substance by precipitation followed by filtration. You should include the following elements in your answer:

adding dilute hydrochloric acid;
testing to see the precipitation is complete (excess acid);
filtering;

washing the precipitate to remove impurities;
a suitable way of drying the aspirin.

The explanation you give for your method being suitable should point out how it achieves the required objective, i.e. getting all the possible aspirin, and getting it pure and dry.

(b) You should use this part of the question to show what you understand about the principles which underlie precipitation and filtration. Some aspirin would be lost due to incomplete precipitation, some due to it passing through the filter paper, and some due to it being carried away in the washings.

Questions drawn from many areas (see pages 88–92)

Structured questions

1 *(a)* sugar beet
   (b) (i) 'aqueous solution'
      (ii) Provides the enzyme which acts as a catalyst.
      (iii) Boiling kills the enzyme.
      (iv) fermentation
      (v) Helps the bread to rise.
   (c) A renewable energy source is one that we can always make more of.
   (d) Less carbon monoxide would be produced. There would be no need for lead compounds.
   (e) In order to make 'meths' dangerous to drink. Methanol is a poison. This allows methylated spirits to be sold without the usual level of taxes on strong ethanol.

2 *(a)* Y is hydrogen
      Z is chlorine
   (b) (i) exactly 7
      (ii) The ions present are $Na^+(aq)$, $H^+(aq)$, $OH^-(aq)$ and $Cl^-(aq)$. Electrolysis removes some H^+ and Cl^-, leaving an excess of $OH^-(aq)$ ions over $H^+(aq)$. This is an alkaline solution.
      (iii) sodium hydroxide
   (c) (i) 'aqueous solution'
      (ii) a green gas (chlorine)
   (d) (i) Substance A could be lead(II) bromide.
         Substance B could be sulphur.
      (ii) covalent (molecular) bonds
      (iii) metallic bonding
      (iv) ions
   (e) (i) At the cathode: hydrogen
         At the anode: oxygen

The cations present are Al^{3+}(aq) and H^+(aq).

H^+ is discharged in preference to Al^{3+}.

The anions present are OH^-(aq) and SO_4^{2-}(aq).

OH^- is discharge in preference to SO_4^{2-}.

(ii) To lower the melting point. (This lowers the cost of the process.)

3 *(a)* (i) Y (ii) X (iii) V, W

(b) They move more and more rapidly, until the forces of attraction holding them together in the lattice structure are overcome. The particles become freer to move about, forming small groups which keep changing in their composition by breaking up and forming again.

(c) (i) As a solid. Continuing the trend for the other elements in the group, its melting point and boiling point would both be above room temperature.

(ii) 71 (53 + 18)

(iii) Z^- (Atomic numbers are 9, 17, 35 etc.
So electronic structures must be 2, 7 then 2, 8, 7 etc.
So each element needs to gain one electron to obtain the inert gas structure.)

(d) $2M \ + \ W_2 \ \rightarrow 2MW$

0.46g   0.71g

Relative atomic mass of W is 35.5

$\therefore$ Relative molecular mass is $2 \times 35.5 = 71$

$2 \times$ relative atomic mass of M react with relative molecular mass of X

46g of M must react with 71g of X

$\therefore$ 46g is $2 \times$ relative atomic mass of M

$\therefore$ Relative atomic mass of M = 23

Free-response question

(a) Mass of metal = 5.55 − 4.75g = 0.8g

Mass of metal iodide = 8.67 − 4.75g = 3.92g

$\therefore$ Mass of iodine reacting = 3.92 − 0.8g = 3.12g

$\therefore$ 3.12g of iodine react with 0.8g of metal.

Relative number of particles M: I

is $\dfrac{0.8}{65} : \dfrac{3.12}{127}$

= 0.0123 : 0.0246

=   1 : 2

$\therefore$ Formula = MI_2.

(b) You are being asked to state what you know about the relative reactivity of the halogens, and to explain what you understand about the underlying principles of the chemistry which is involved.

You should start by listing the halogens as they appear in the Periodic Table, and stating the order of relative reactivity.

Explain what you know about the ability of some halogens to displace from aqueous solution the halide ions of other halogens. Describe any reactions which you have seen, stating how you decided what the reaction was that was taking place. Give any chemical equations. Try to explain what you can about the relative reactivity of the halogens in terms of the structure of their atoms.

SECTION 7
Preparing for the GCSE examination

'KNOW, UNDERSTAND AND CAN DO'

Remember that GCSE chemistry will be designed to help you to show what you know, understand and can do.

You have seen in this book how the assessment objectives for GCSE chemistry have been translated in the different syllabuses into the content of the subject. You have seen how the examinations will be put together, and the type of questions that you will meet. Make sure you know exactly what to expect for each examination paper you take. Is it multiple-choice, structured or free-response? Get yourself in the right frame of mind.

Look back now at the descriptions of performance at different levels given on page 35. You can see the different skills that the examination is looking for. Look again at the assessment objectives on page 17. Now you can begin to see what you have to do in the GCSE examination. You can see the kinds of knowledge and skill that will be expected of you.

The assessment of coursework in GCSE chemistry was described in detail in Section 4 of this book. You should know the assessment criteria that will be used to assess your own coursework – your teacher will almost certainly tell you. So you should know exactly what will be expected of you when your coursework is being assessed. It will be up to you to show the various skills, understanding and practical abilities that your teacher will be looking for.

So, make sure you know how you are going to be assessed.

REVISION

Nobody can go into an examination without having prepared themselves and then expect to do themselves justice. Getting the best grade you can in an examination is a skill, made up of two parts: preparing yourself in the best way and getting the most out of the examination paper on the day itself. But how to prepare? What does 'revision' mean?

When you 'revise, you are giving yourself the equipment to do well in the examination. You make sure that your ideas are clear and that you can remember facts when you need them in the examination. Revision makes the examination easy.

So you have to learn facts, and get your ideas clear, when you revise. What is the best way of doing this? There are some simple rules which you can follow that will help. They won't make your revision any easier, enjoyable or effortless. But they will make it more successful.

Rule 1: Give yourself plenty of time

It is no good trying to revise for an important examination like GCSE the night before. By then it's too late. Most people would say you need to start your revision six to eight weeks before the examinations. This is long enough to give you time to do what you have to do, but not so long that you are mentally exhausted and can't think in the examination.

Rule 2: Make a plan

You will get more out of your time if you have worked out in advance what you are going to do each day. That way, you will have given each subject the right amount of time at the end. A plan is also a good discipline. It is something to make yourself stick to.

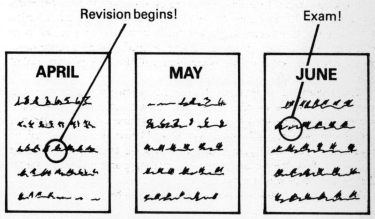

Give yourself plenty of time

Rule 3: Frequent beats lengthy

There is good scientific evidence from learning experiments that you can retain more information about something if you have come across it several times briefly, than if you have pored over it once for many hours. So split your revision sessions into work on more than one subject. This way you get two advantages – you 'revisit' each subject frequently, and each session is more productive because you don't get bogged down mentally looking at the same subject. Probably three different subjects in a two-hour session is about right.

You should also timetable some breaks. Believe it or not, your brain needs periods to consolidate. Having a break can actually help you learn, as well as preventing you from getting the feeling suddenly that life is no fun!

So your revision timetable might look something like this:

Monday	Tuesday	Wednesday	Thursday	Friday	Saturday
English	Chemistry	Physics	French	Physics	Chemistry
Physics	Maths	English	Chemistry	DISCO	English
Maths	History	French	Maths		TENNIS

and so on.

Rule 4: Learn how to learn

Different people find that different ways of learning suit them best. Some need absolute quiet, others need background noise. Not everybody is equally fortunate in the environment they have for their revision, of course, but it is normally possible to find the conditions you need – take your books to a reference library, or to a friend's house if need be. If it's suitable, though, a bedroom is usually the best place to work in.

Some people find that writing out what they are learning helps them. Others read for a while, then try to summarise afterwards in writing. Others can learn from just reading. But always test yourself after a little while – and check back to see how accurate your memory is. Then build in the bits you missed, or remembered inaccurately!

But remember that in GCSE there will be a strong emphasis on your understanding and your ability to explain – not just on what you can remember. So it is important to make sure you have thought through the ideas and the issues you have come across. When you go into the examination you will need to be clear about what you understand and what you think.

EXAMINATIONS

Doing your best in the examination is only partly dependent on preparing yourself well. You then have to perform in such a way that you do yourself justice. Again, there are some simple rules which you should follow.

At the start of any examination, make sure you know how many questions you have to answer. Follow the advice about the amount of time to spend on different sections. *Then spread your time out evenly over the questions*. The first few marks on a question are easy to get. The last few marks are very hard to get.

Make sure you have answered every question

When you are doing multiple-choice questions, *read all the alternatives before you decide on the one you think is right*. Sometimes it seems that alternative A or B is the right answer, when C, D or E is actually a better and right answer, when you compare them all. *Don't try short-cuts*.

Practise doing examination questions, and seeing how the marks are given. There are many examples in this book – you should read them carefully. There are often clues in the wording of questions to what will gain the most marks. For example, 'describe in chemical terms' means the examiner is asking you to give a chemical equation or the equivalent description in words. Only practice will help you to recognise these important aids to getting better marks.

For free-response questions, *always make a short plan* before launching into your answer. Spend five or ten minutes making a list of the things you want to say in answer to the question. Then use this plan to write your answer. This makes your answer more complete, more logical in its order and easier for the examiner to read. Remember he or she will probably have several hundred answers like yours to read – so don't make it too hard by hiding away the points that will get marks in a jungle of needless words. A tired and bored examiner needs help. *So keep to the point*.

One last word – good luck!

(0753)
551037—MOJAR